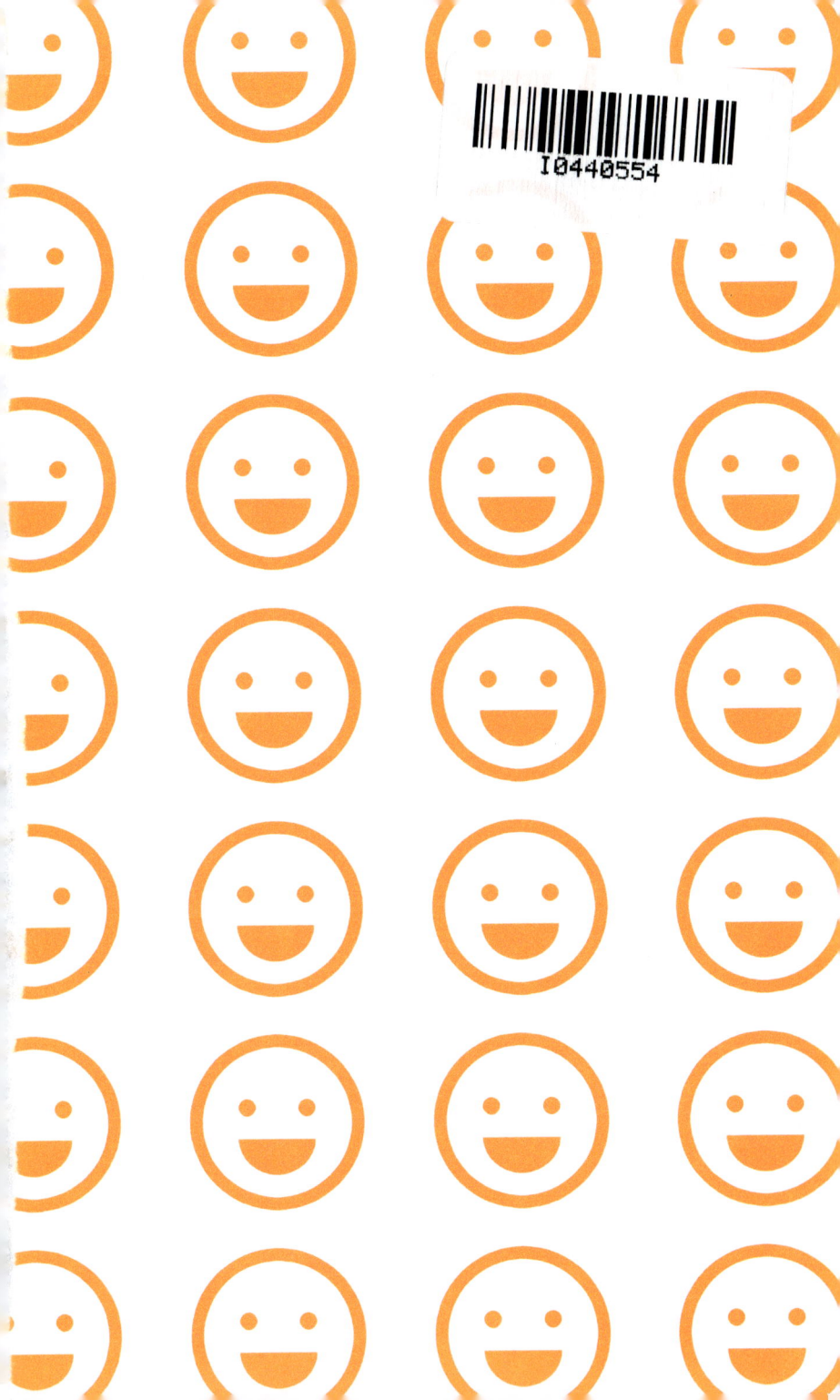

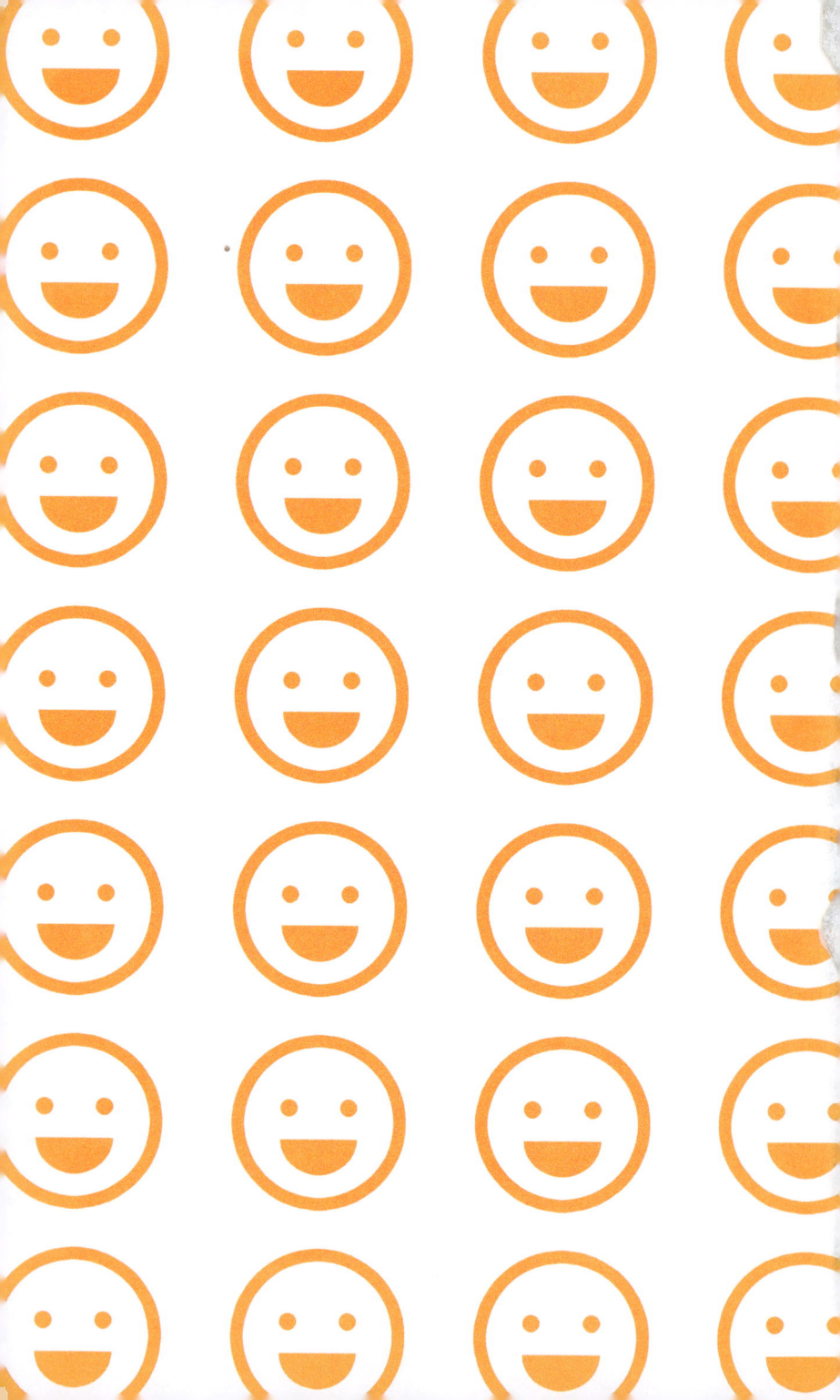

DRIVE FAST DON'T STOP

BOOK SIX SIX SIX

CLASSIC REMISE
BERLIN, GERMANY

TOYOTA HISTORY GARAGE
TOKYO, JAPAN

CUSSLER MUSEUM
COLORADO, U.S.A.

DRIVE FAST DON'T STOP

CLASSIC REMISE

CLASSIC REMISE

CLASSIC REMISE

CLASSIC REMISE

CLASSIC REMISE

CLASSIC REMISE

CLASSIC REMISE

BERLIN, GERMANY

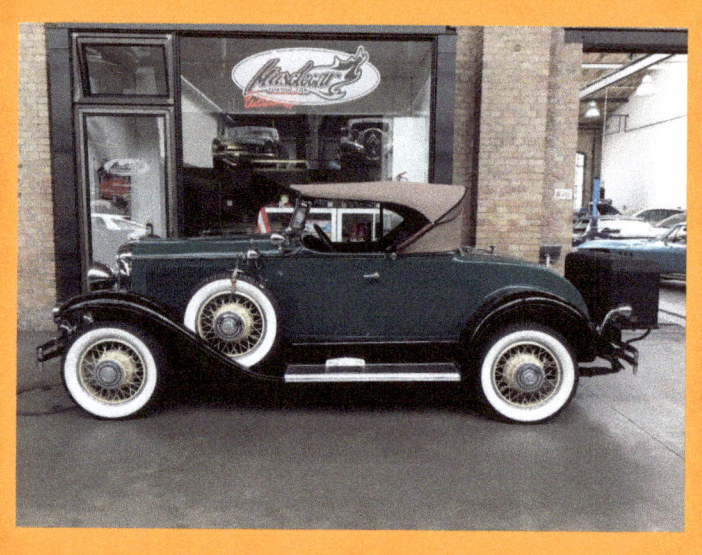

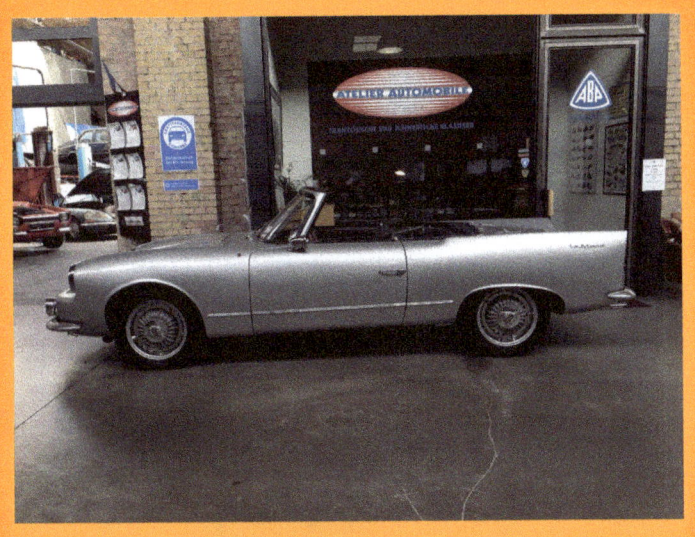

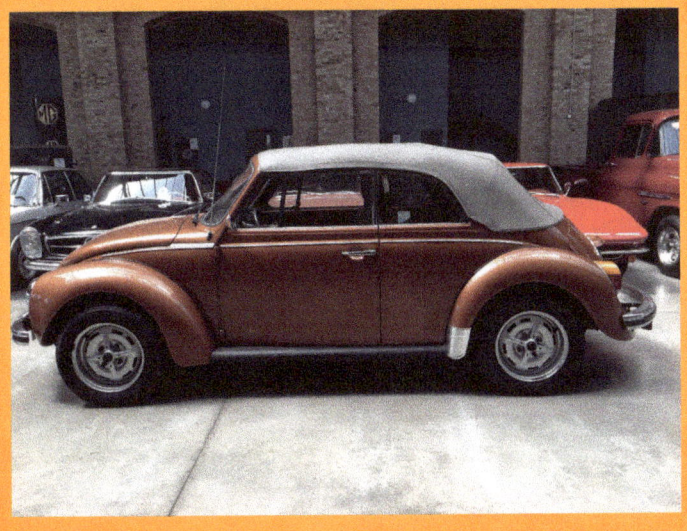

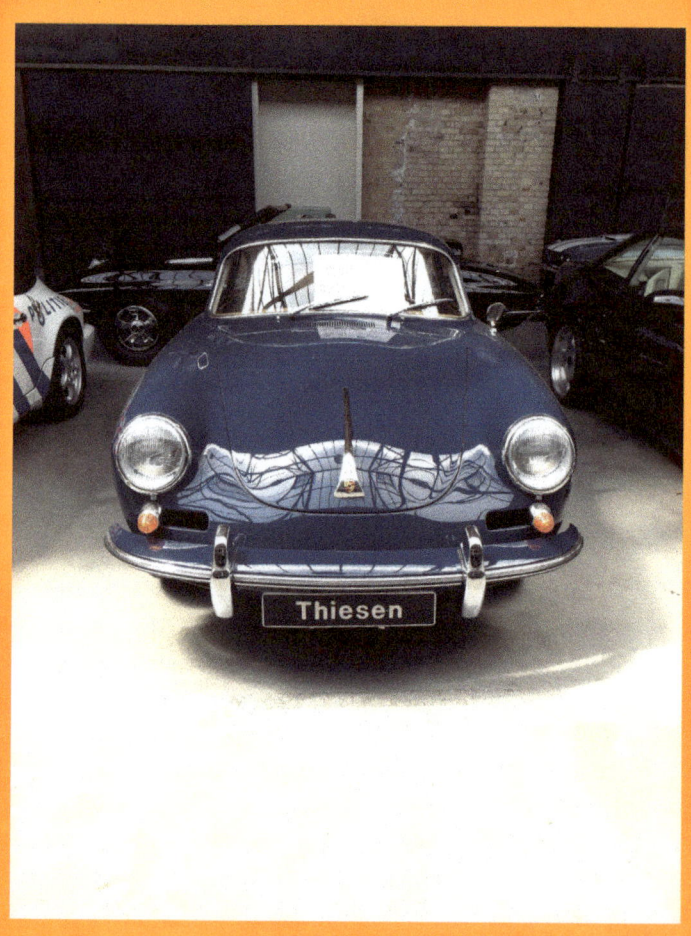

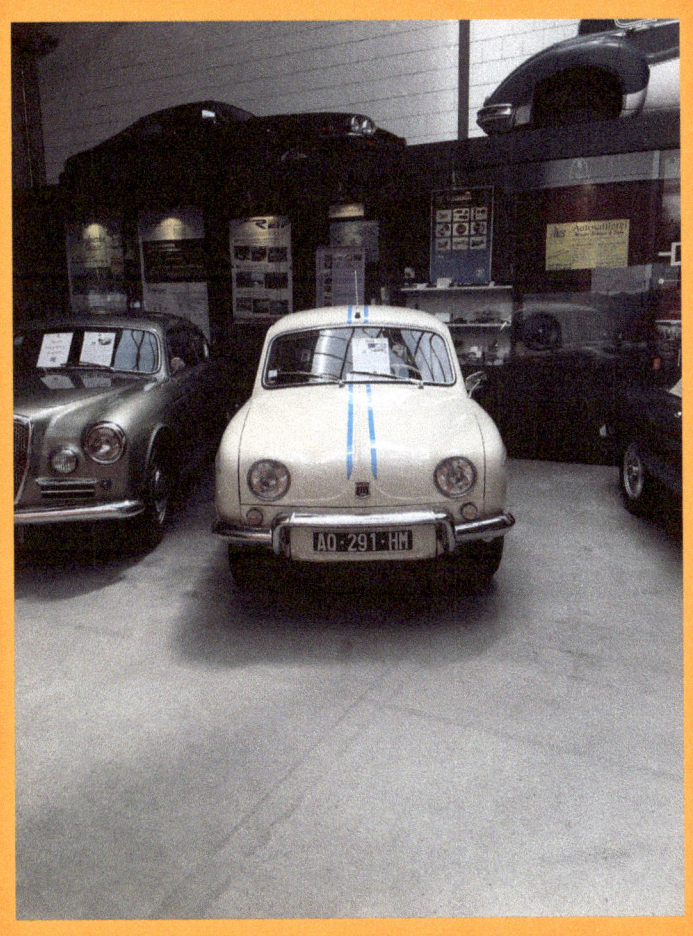

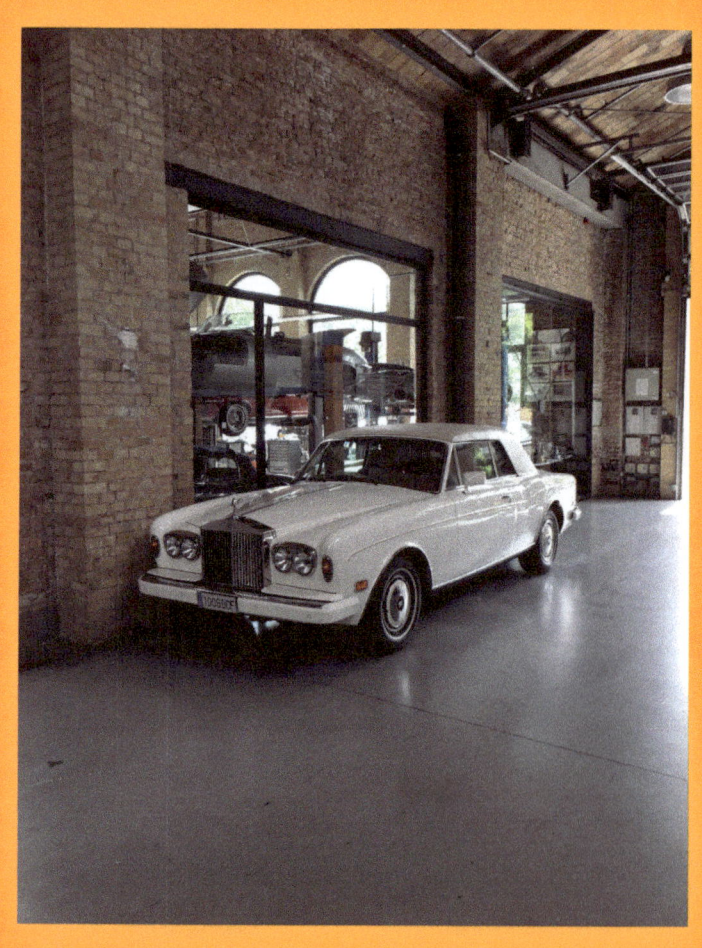

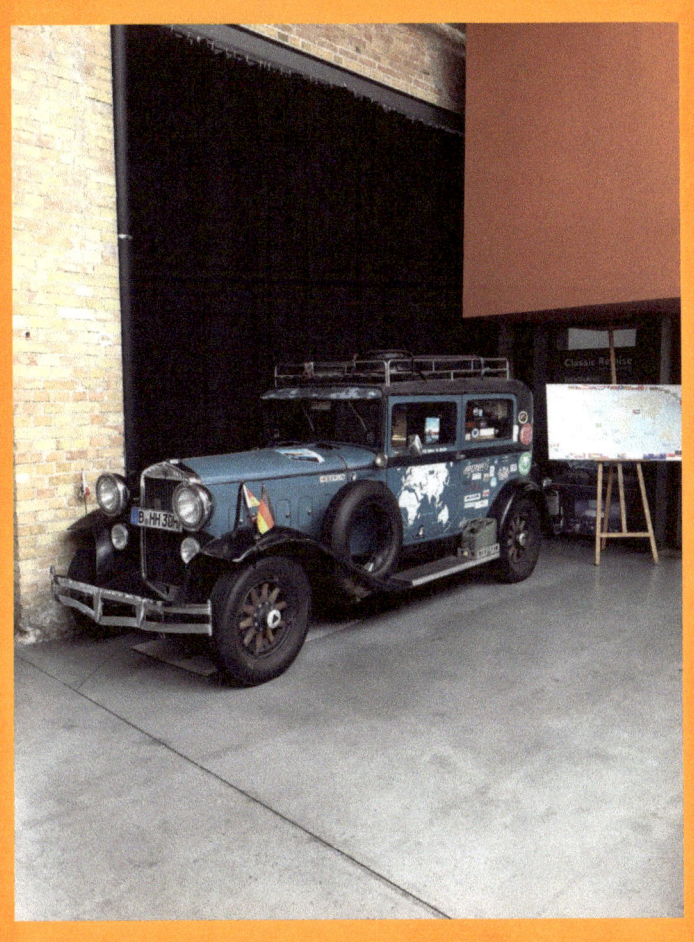

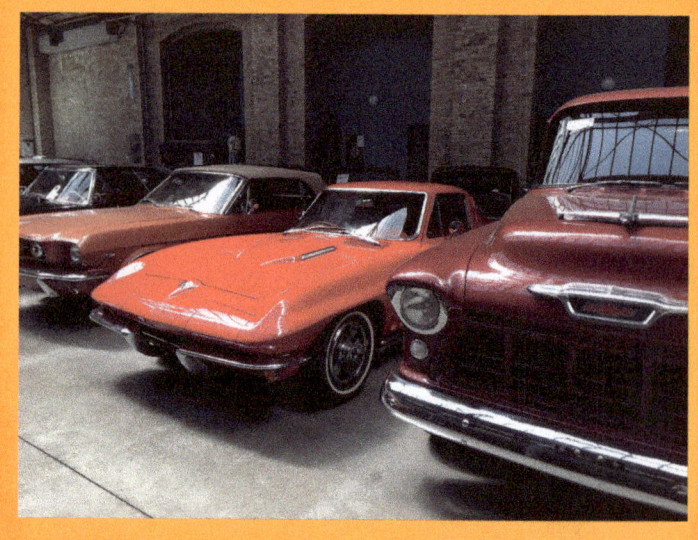

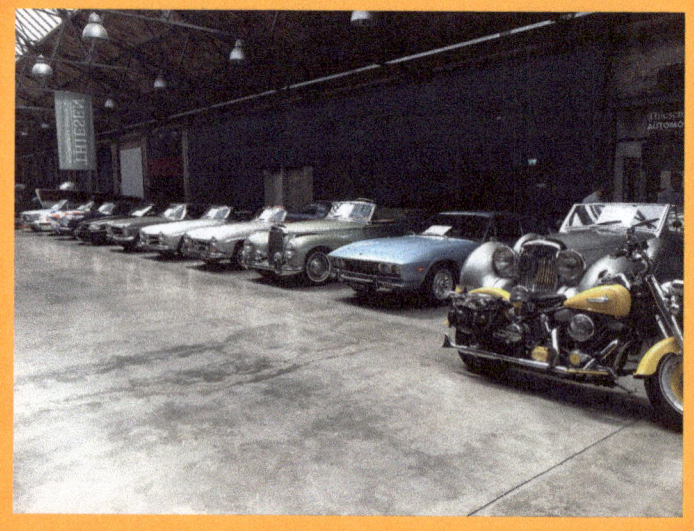

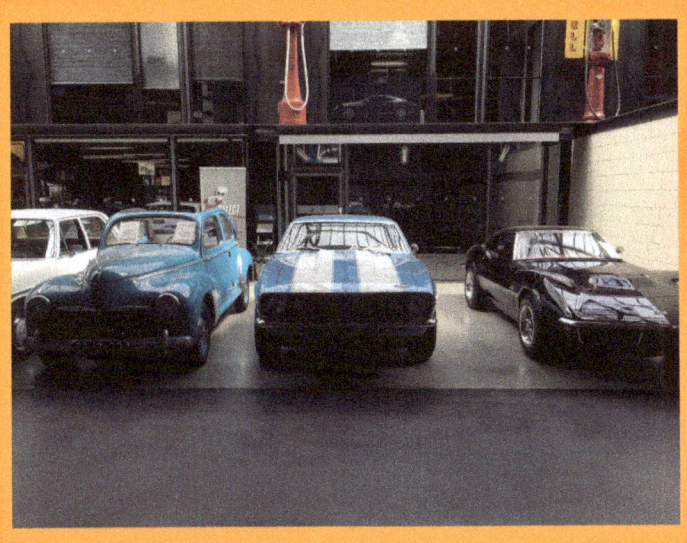

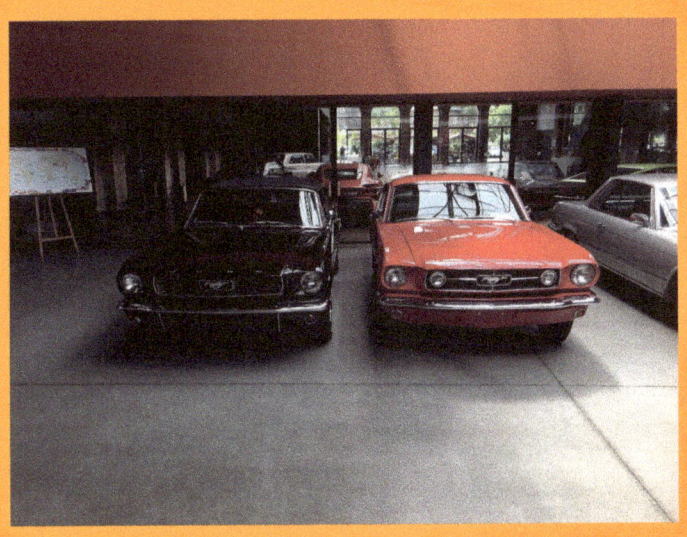

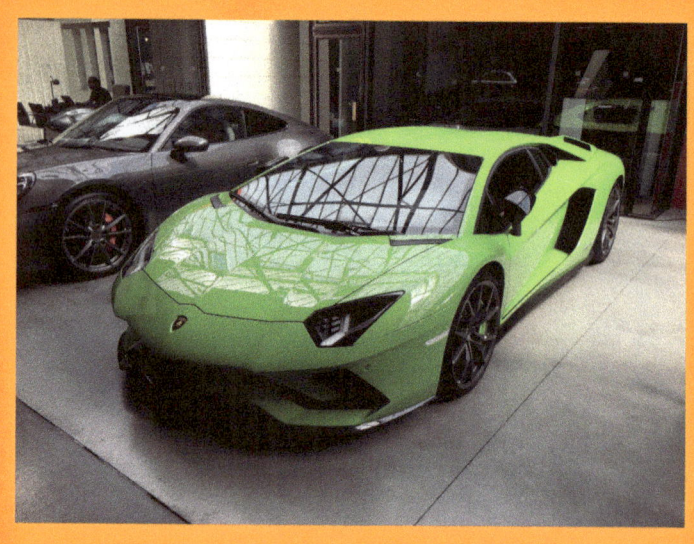

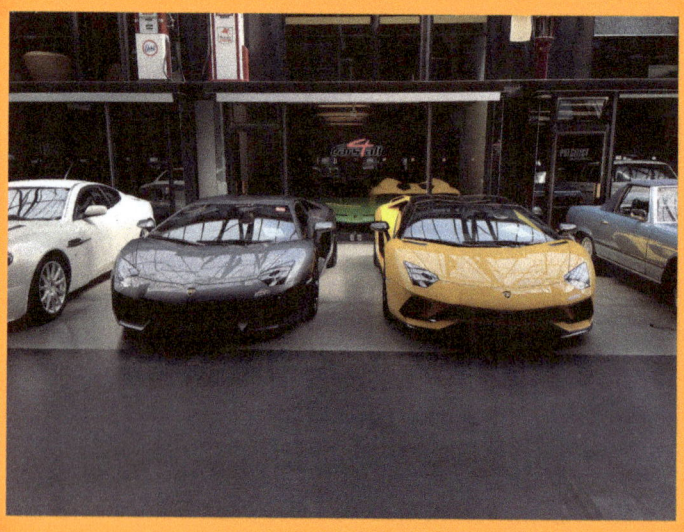

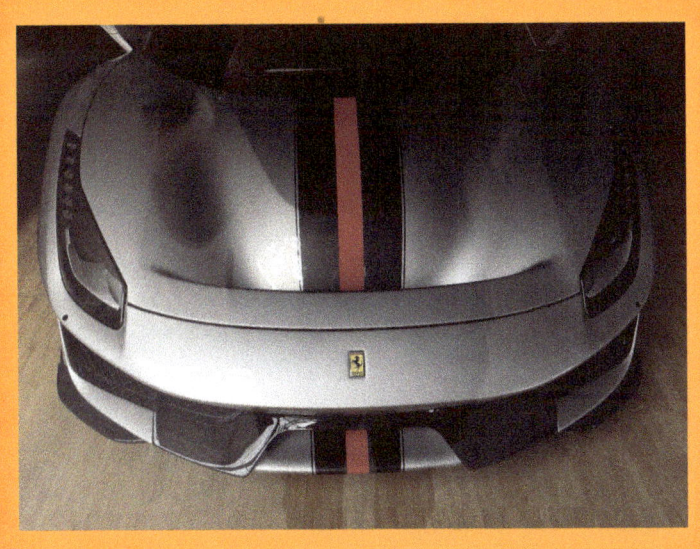

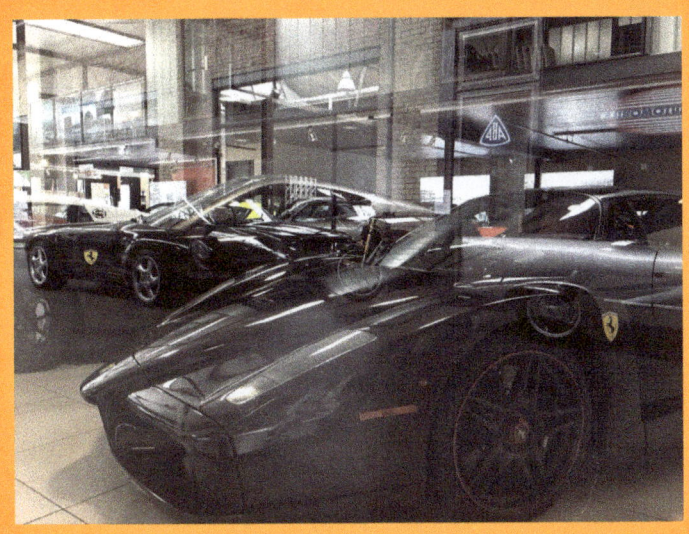

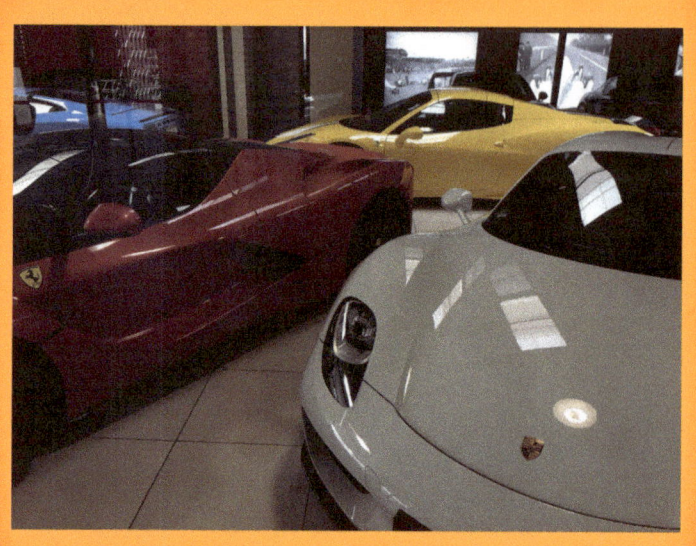

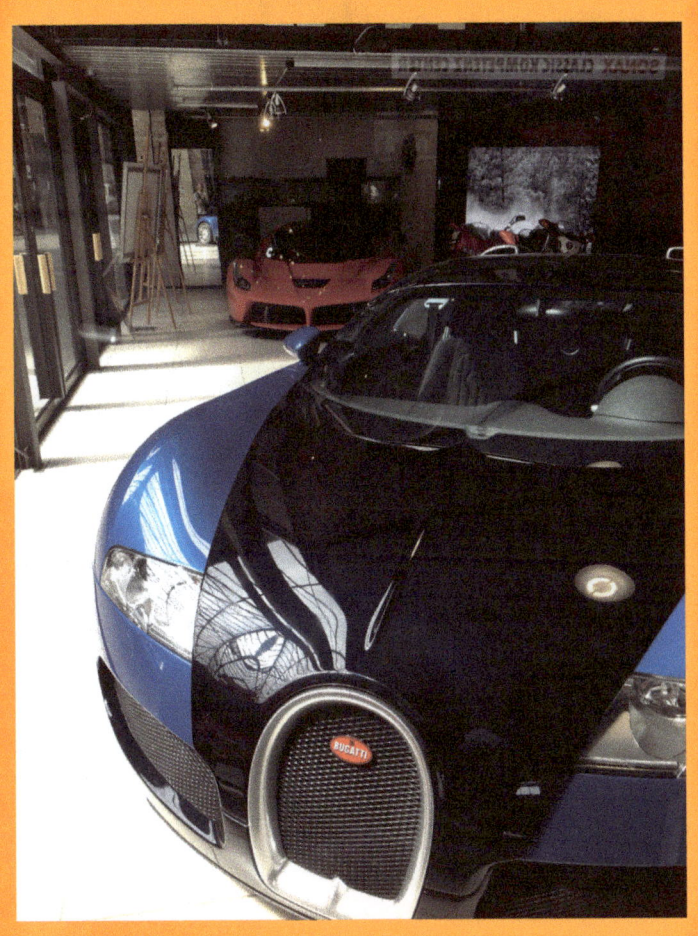

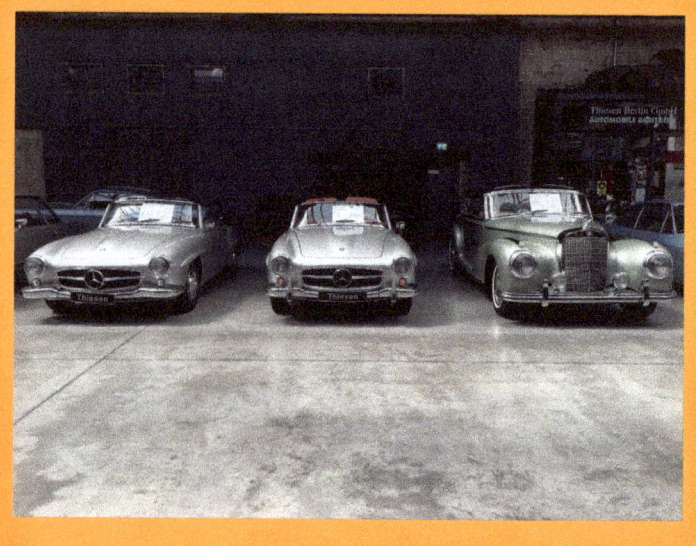

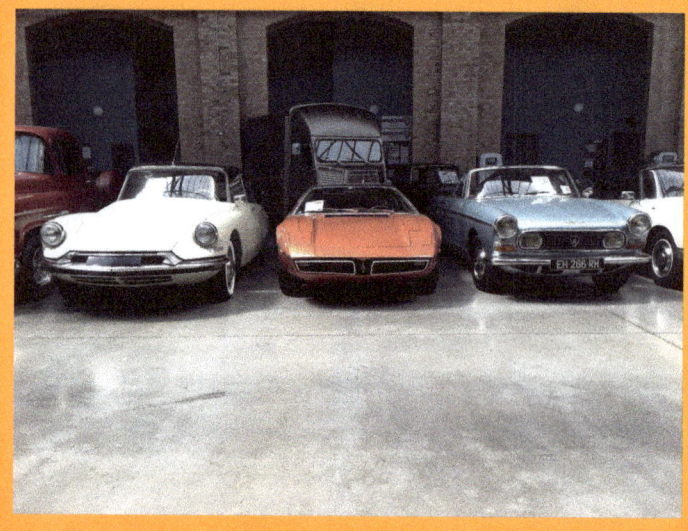

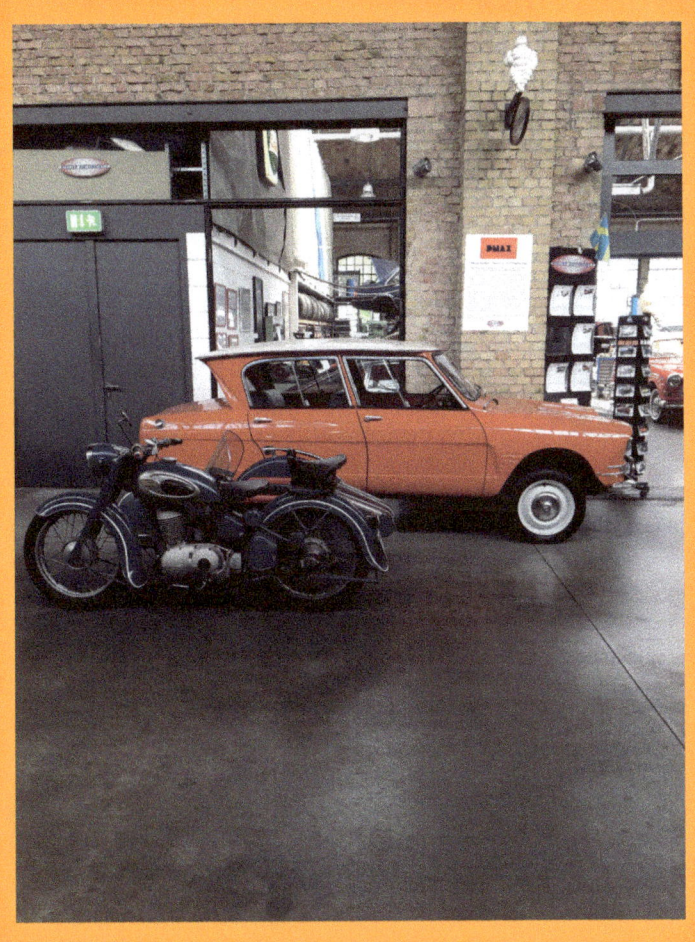

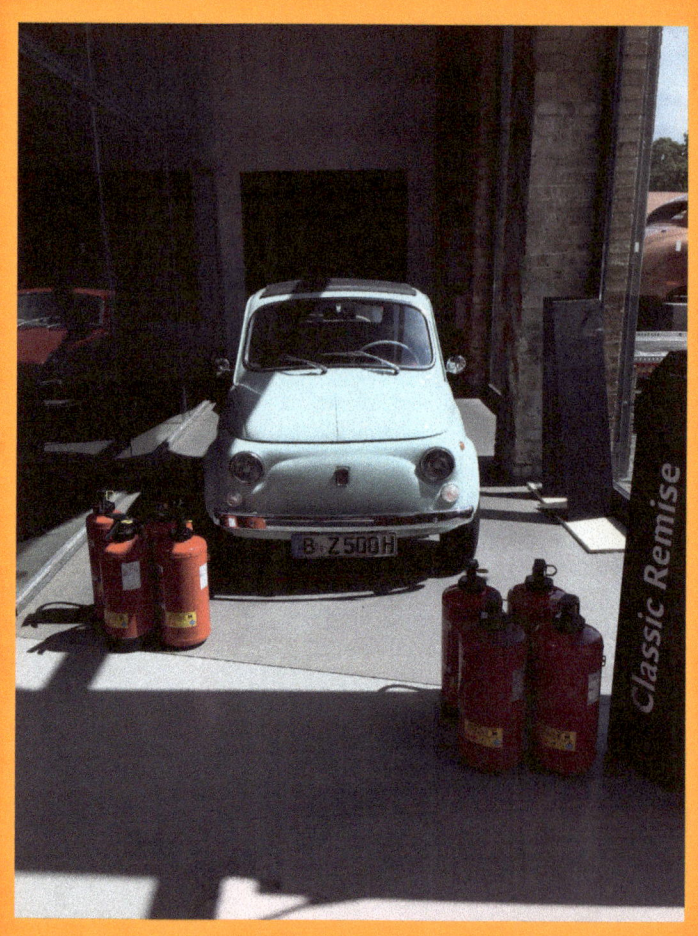

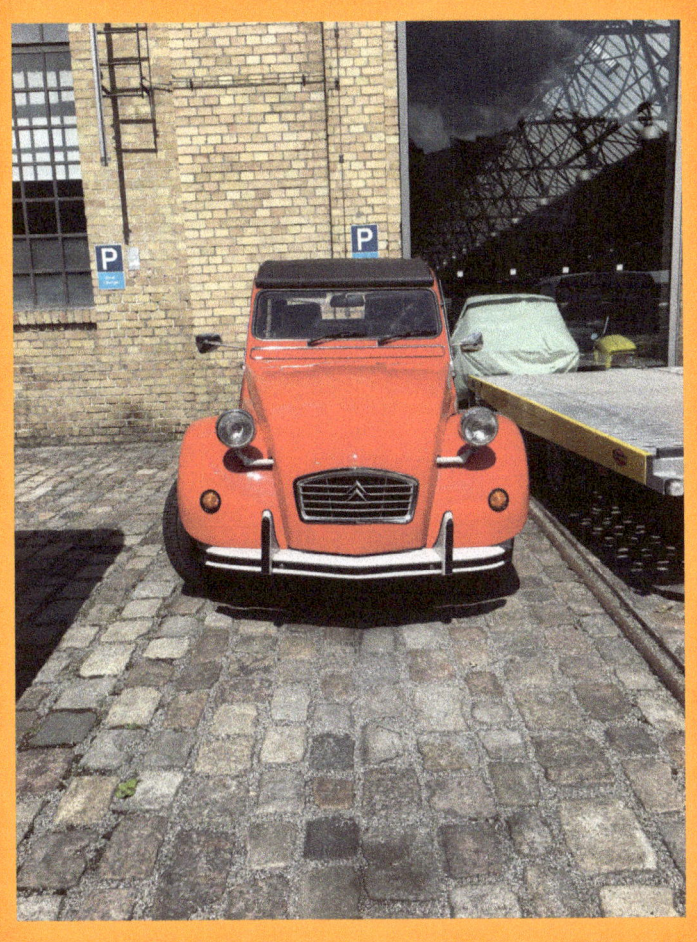

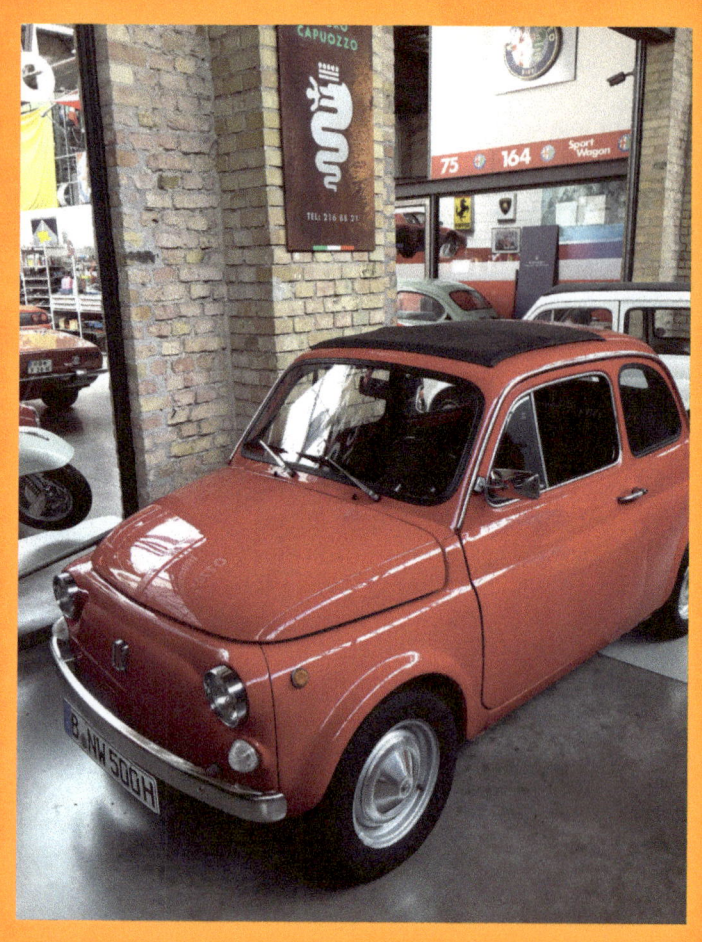

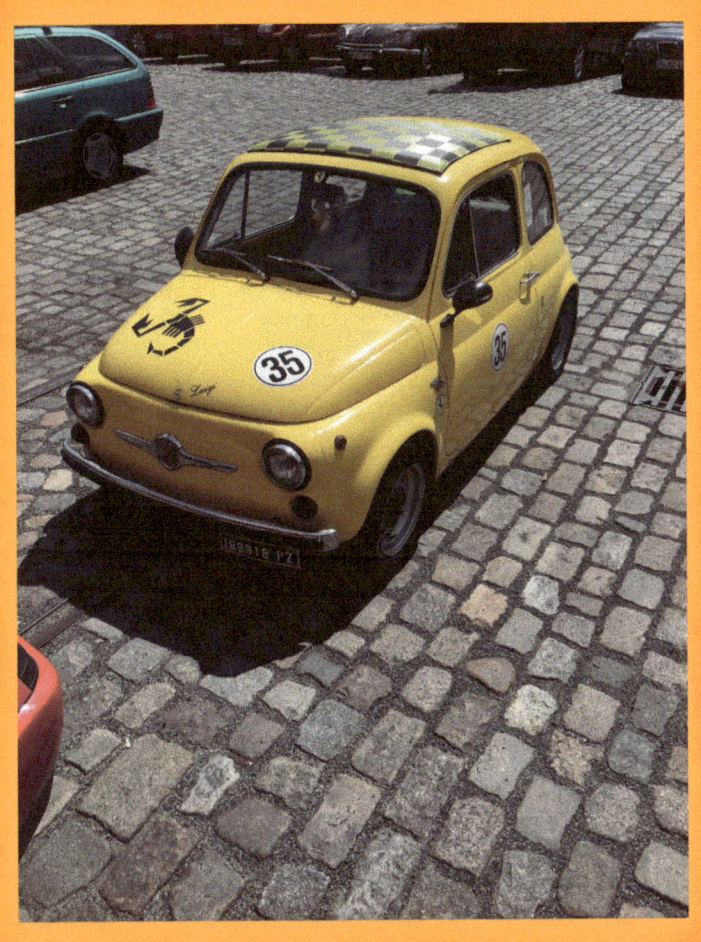

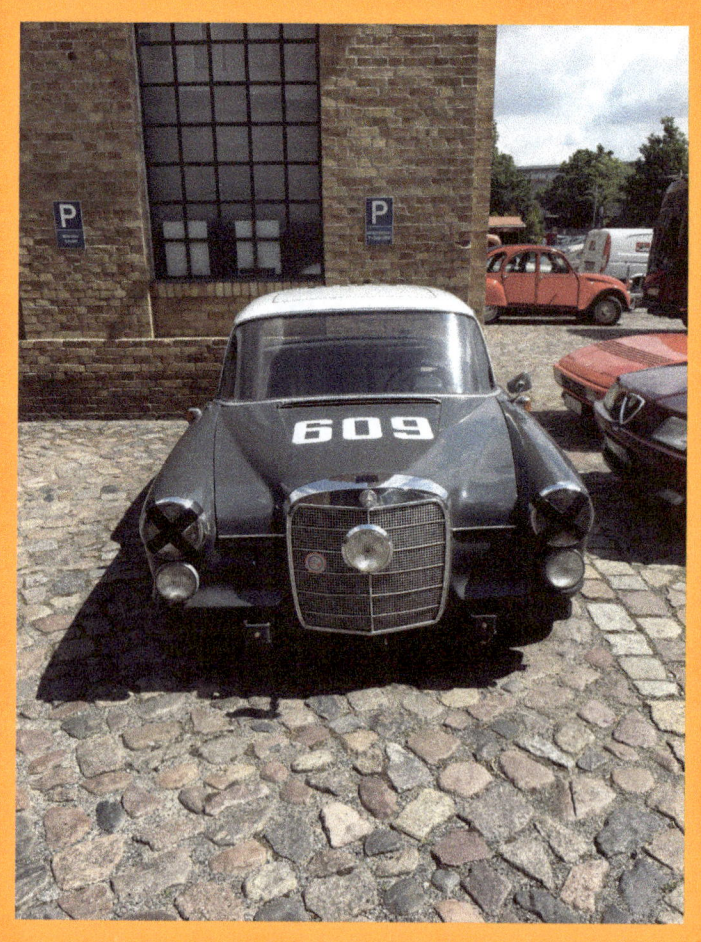

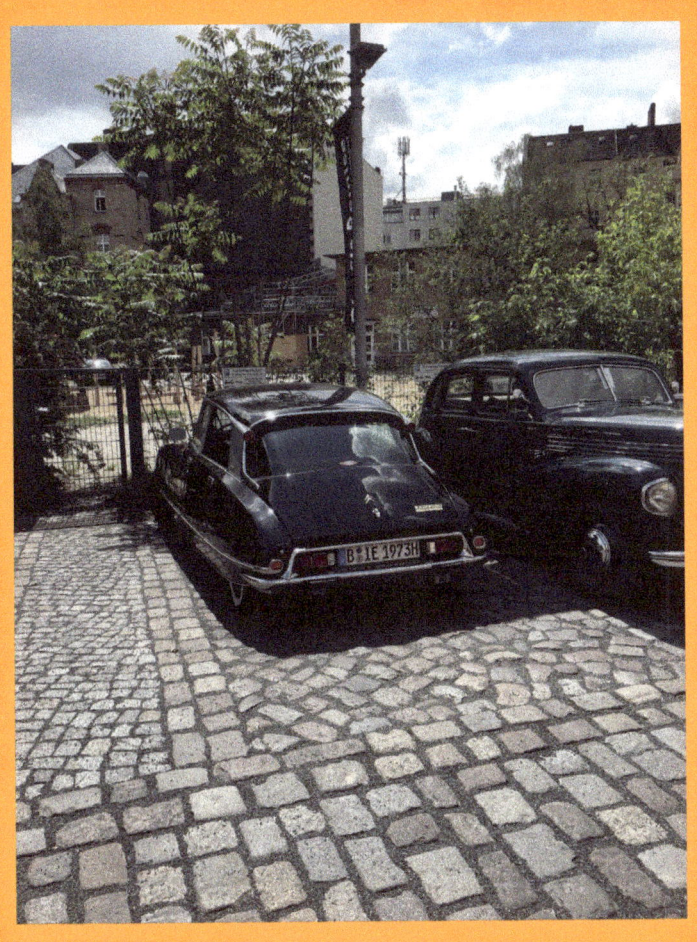

HISTORY G

TA HISTORY G

TA HISTORY GA

OTA HISTORY GA

YOTA HISTORY GARA

TOYOTA HISTORY GARAGE

TOYOTA HISTORY GARAGE

KYO, JAPAN

TOKYO, JAPAN

TOKYO, JAPAN

TOKYO, JAPAN

TOKYO, JAPAN

TOKYO, JAPAN

TOKYO, JAPAN

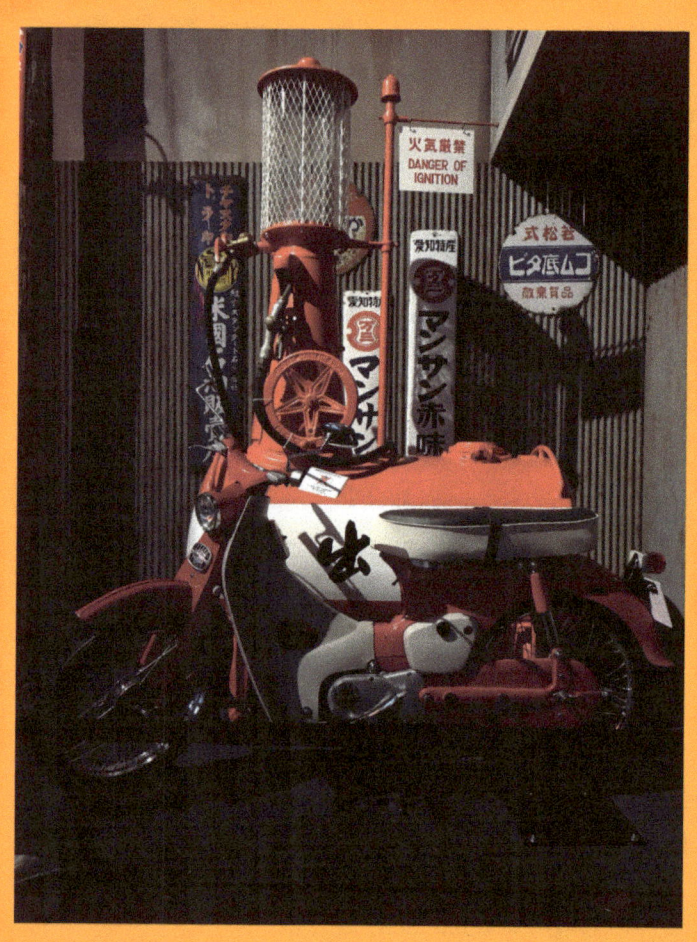

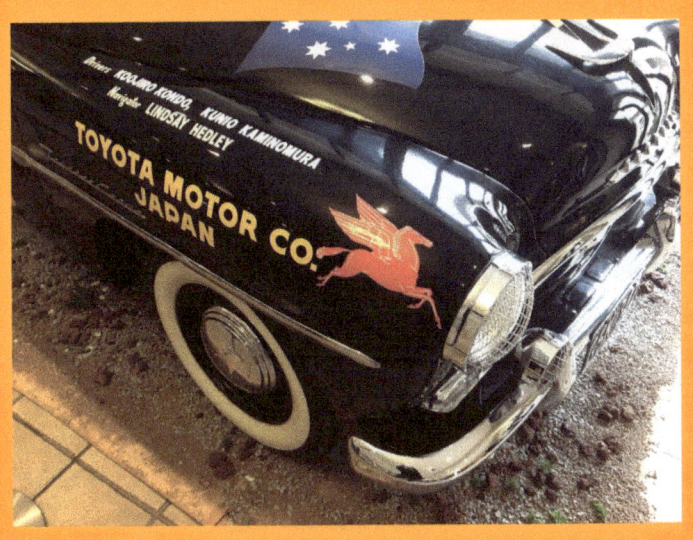

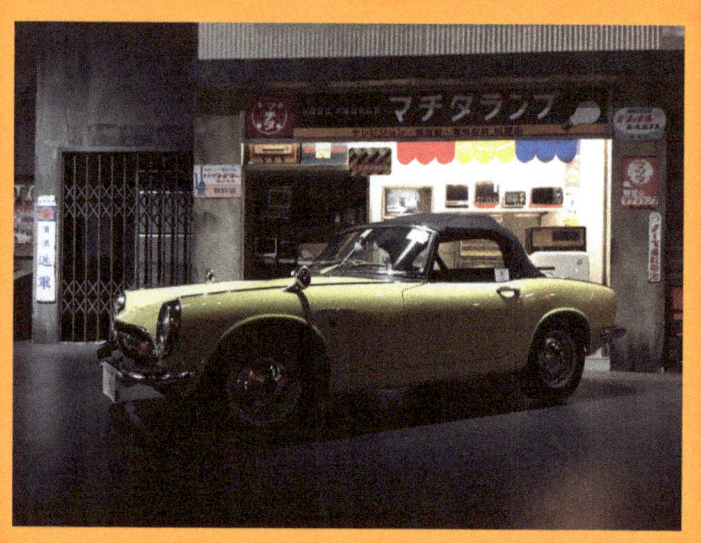

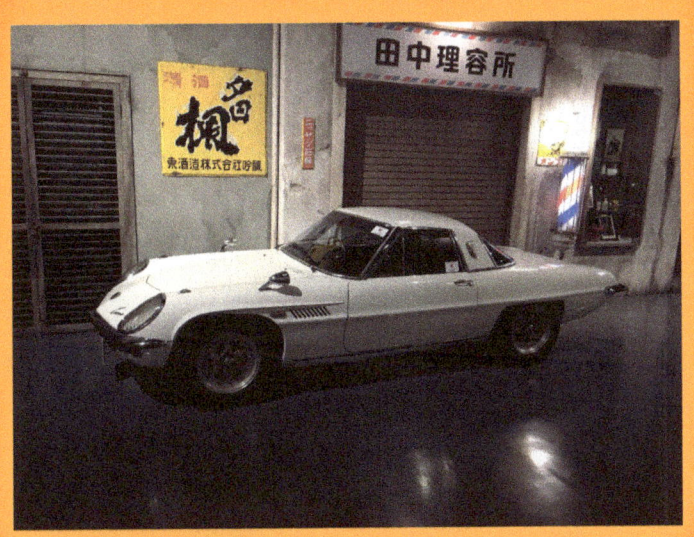

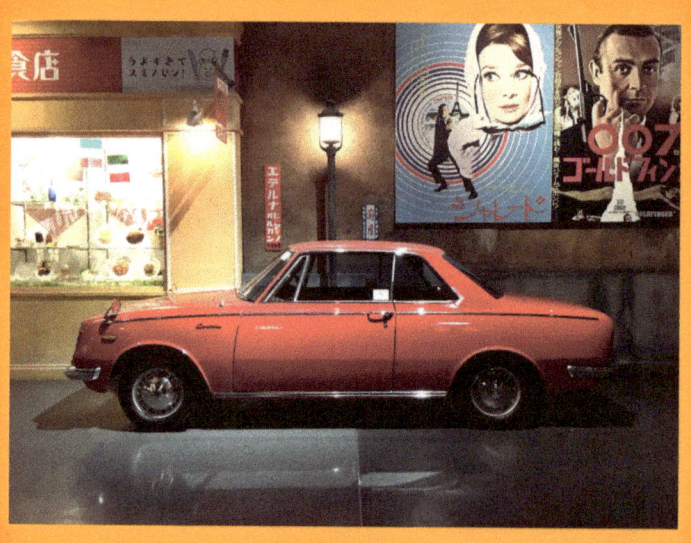
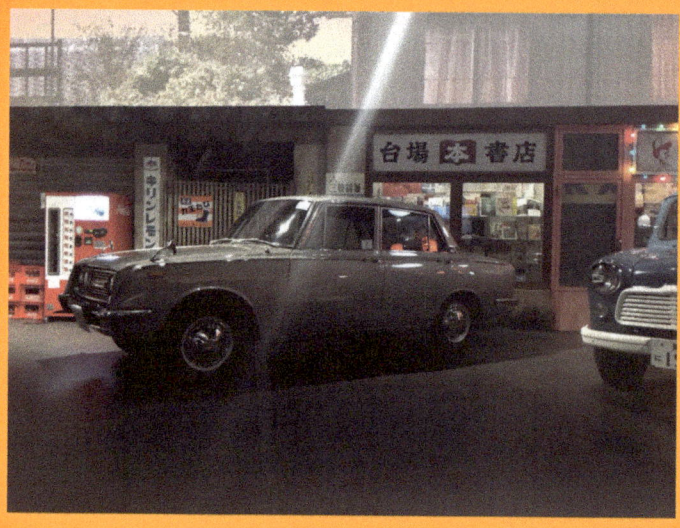

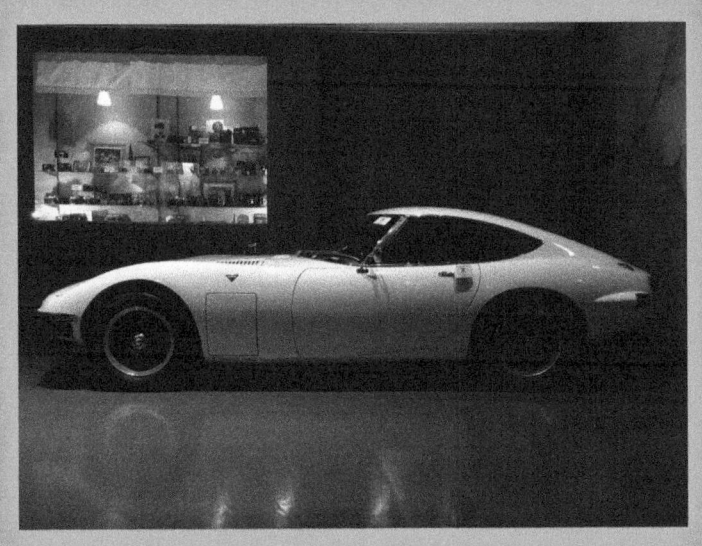

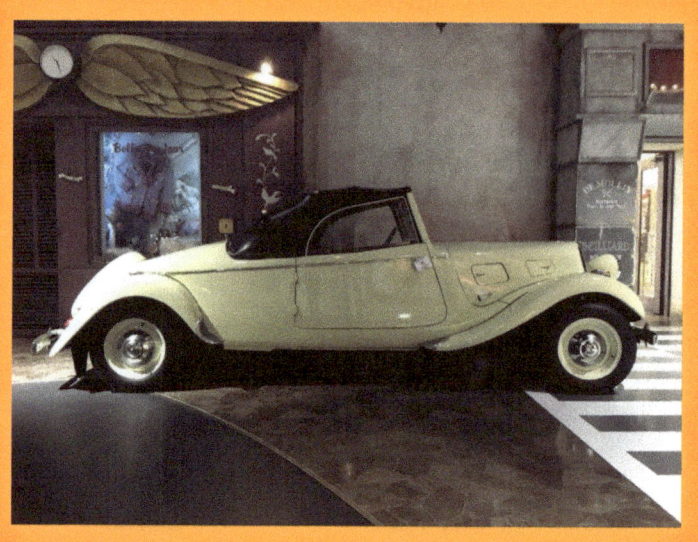

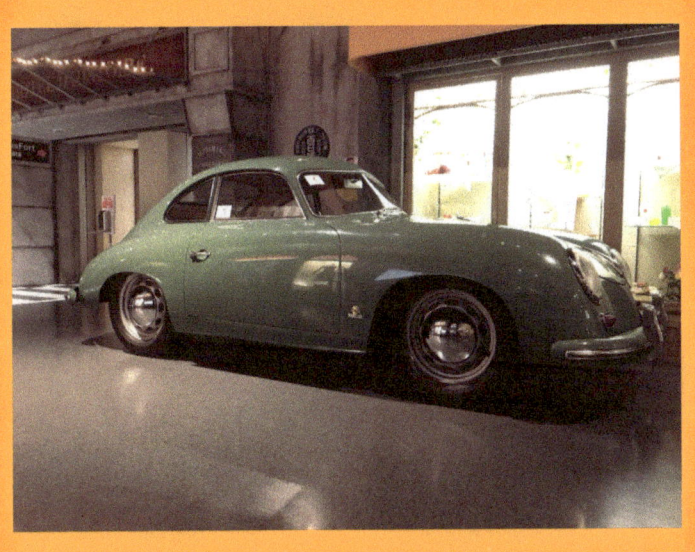

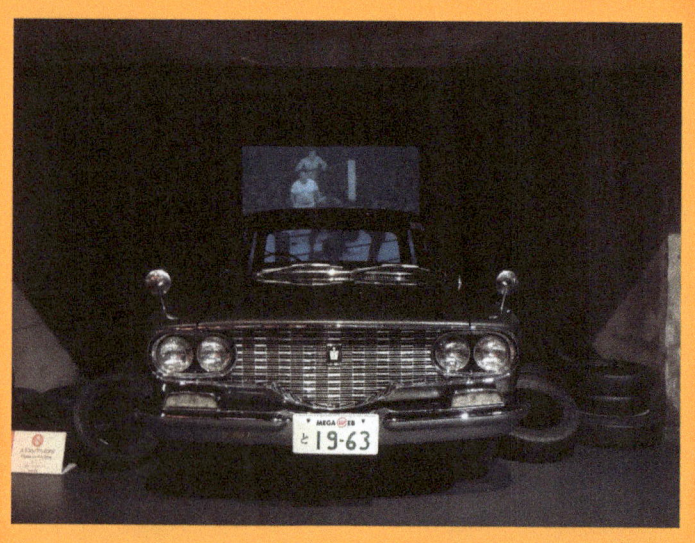

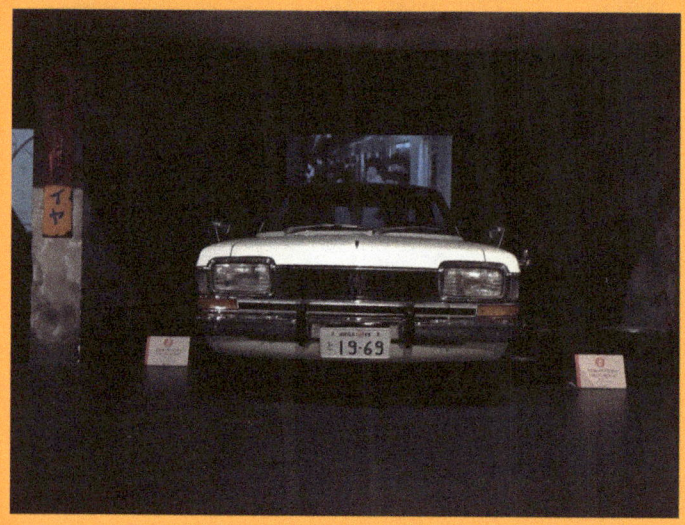

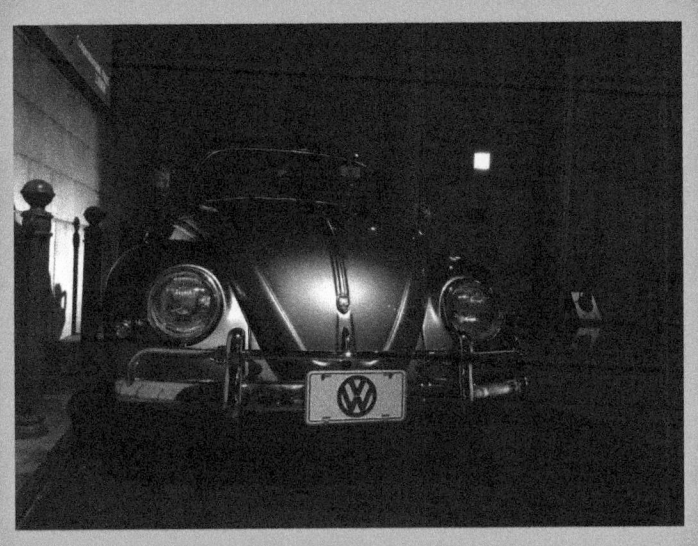

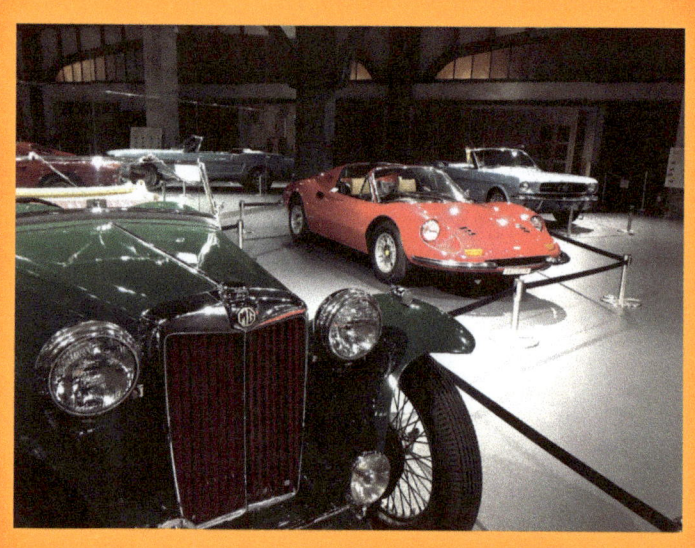

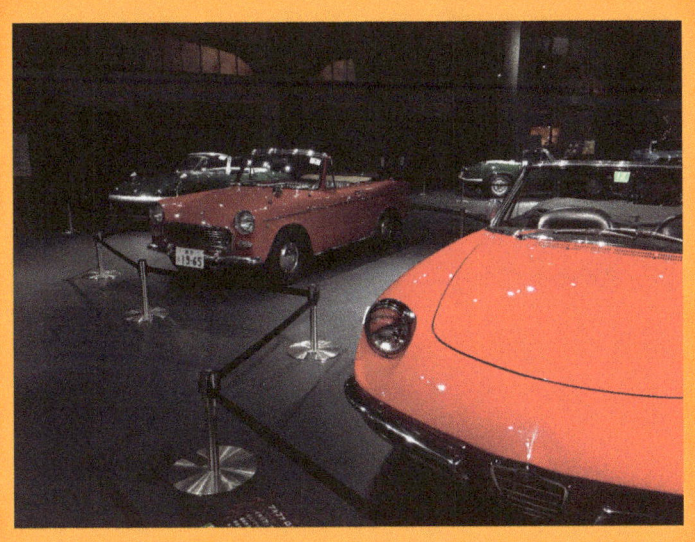

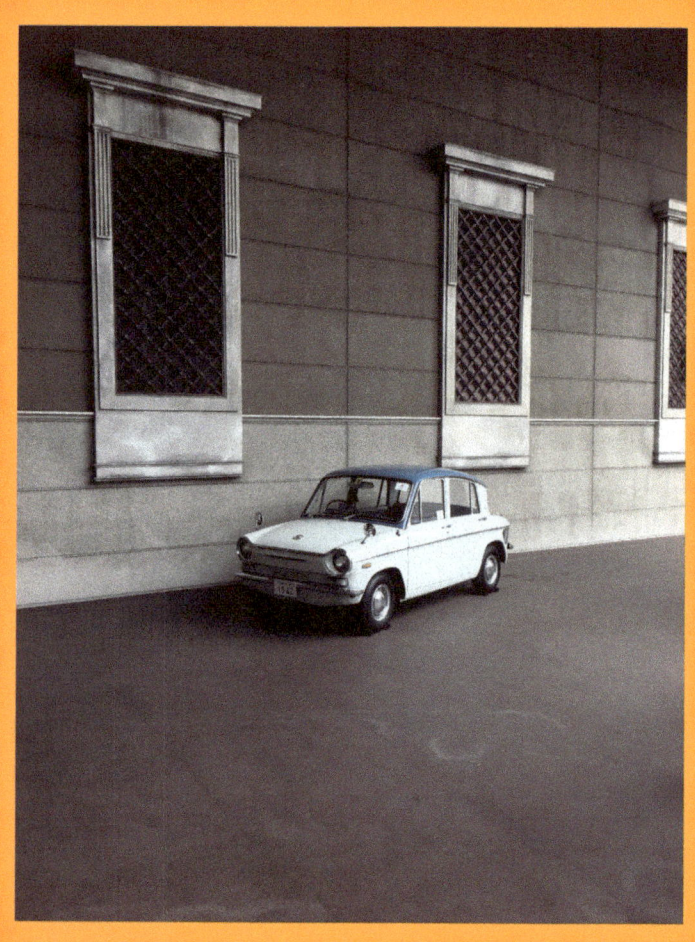

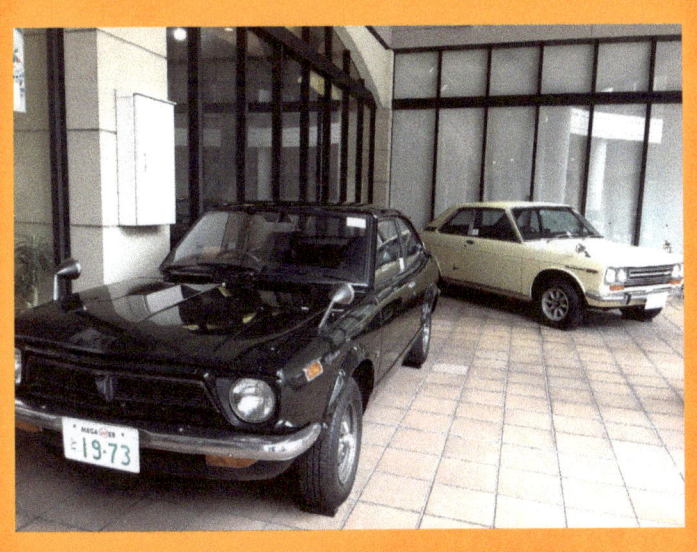

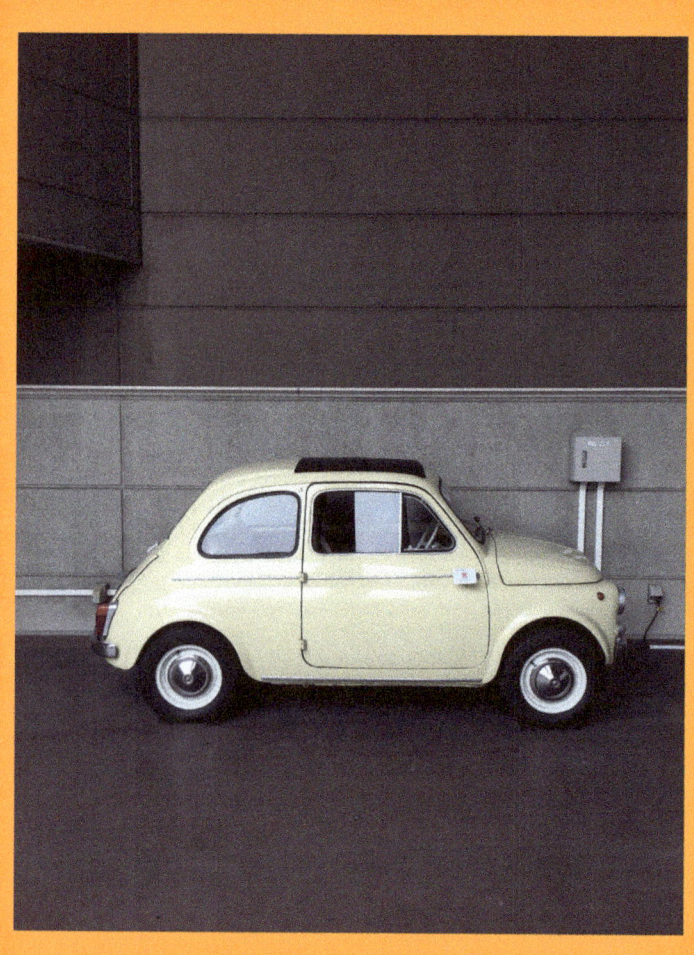

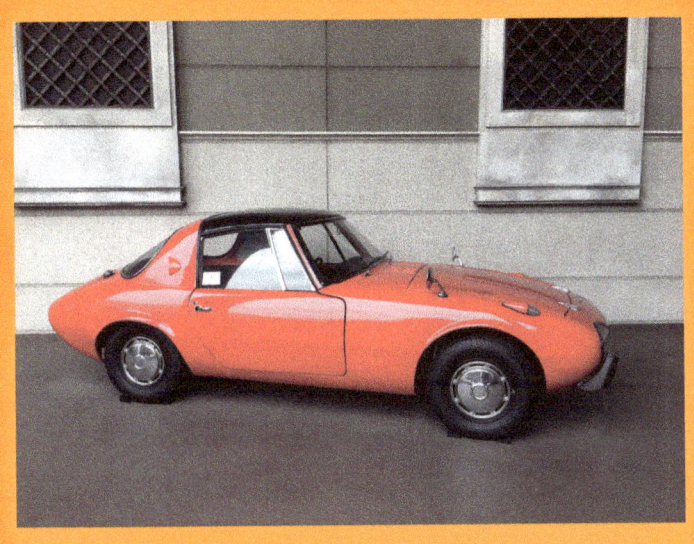

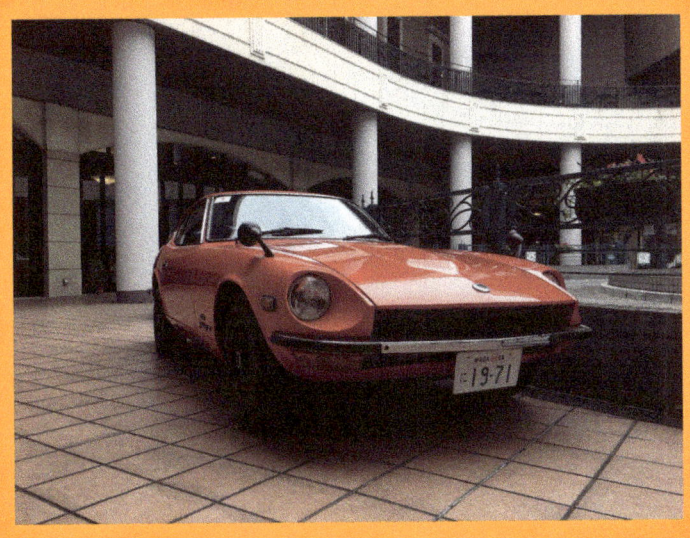

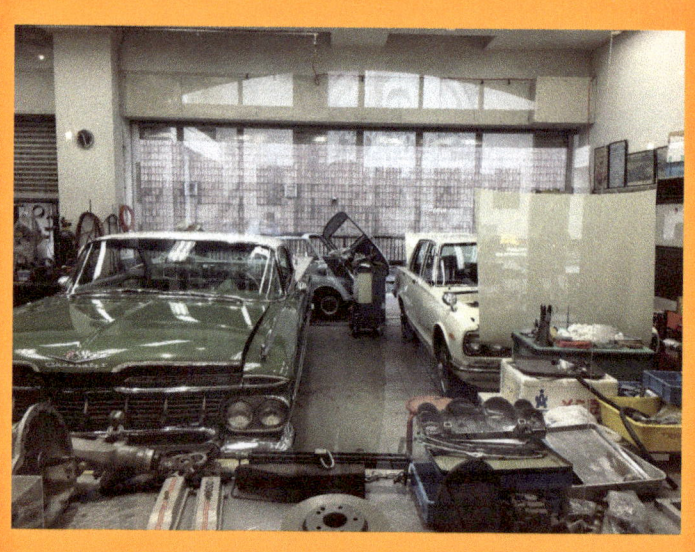

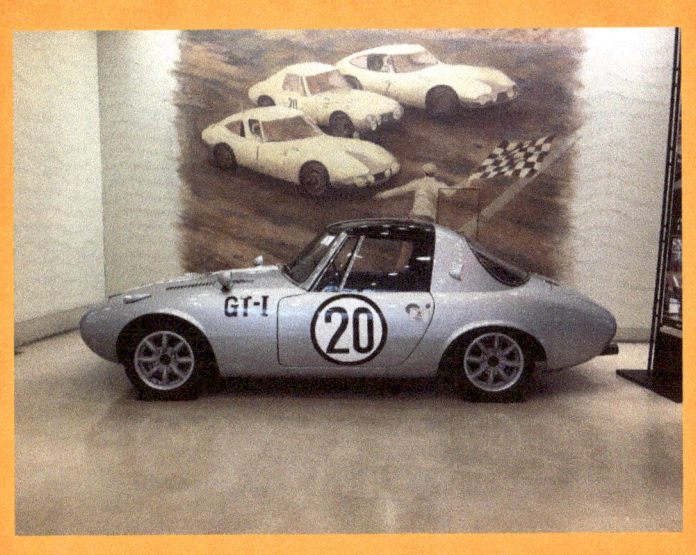

SSLER MUSE

SSLER MUSE

USSLER MUSEU

USSLER MUSEUM

CUSSLER MUSEUM

CUSSLER MUSEUM

CUSSLER MUSEUM

ORADO, U.

ORADO, U.S

LORADO, U.S.

OLORADO, U.S.A

COLORADO, U.S.A.

COLORADO, U.S.A.

COLORADO, U.S.A.

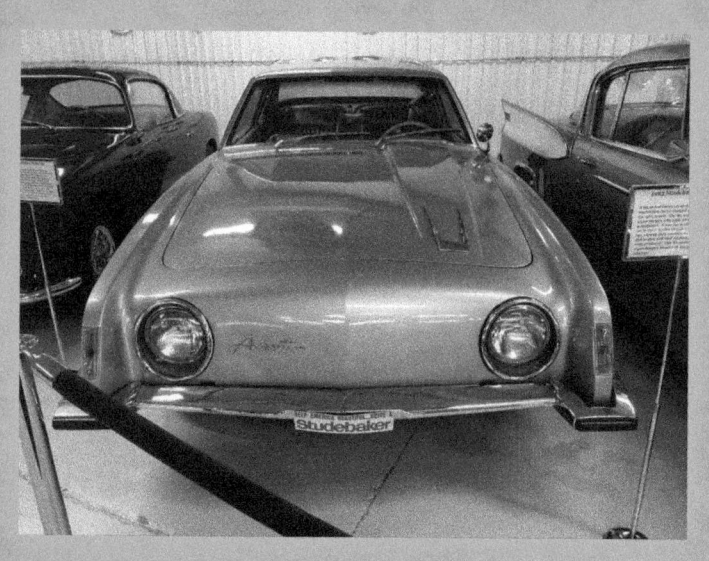

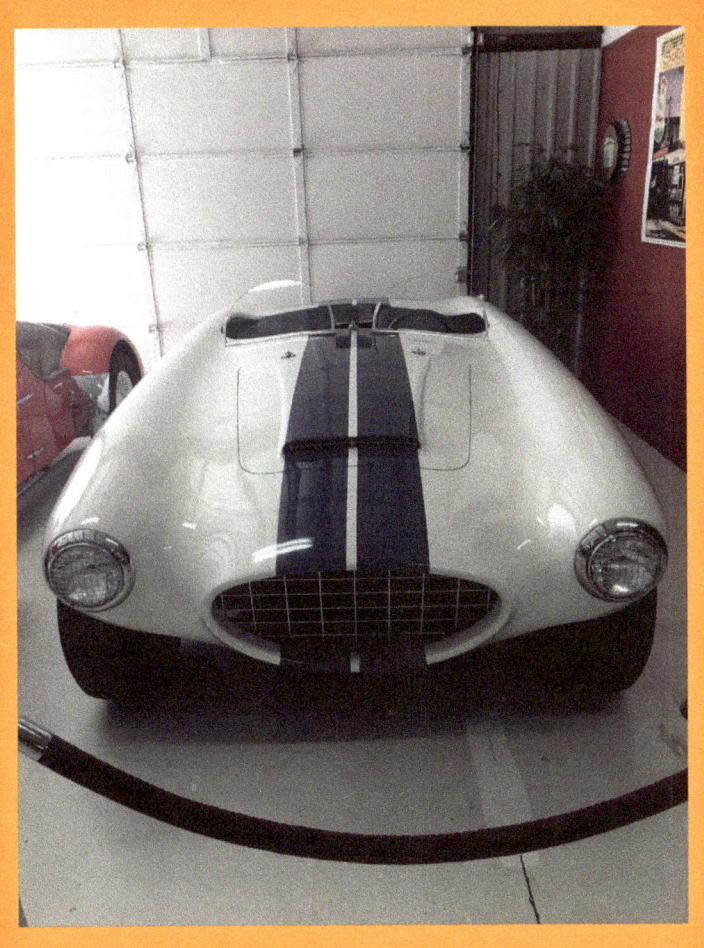

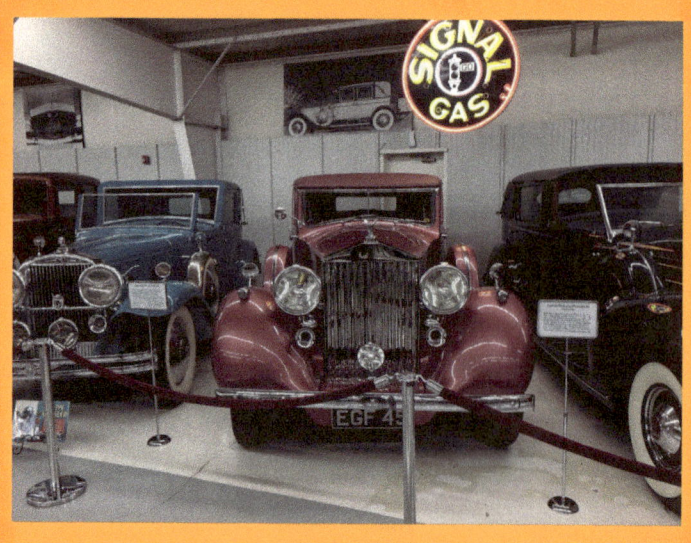

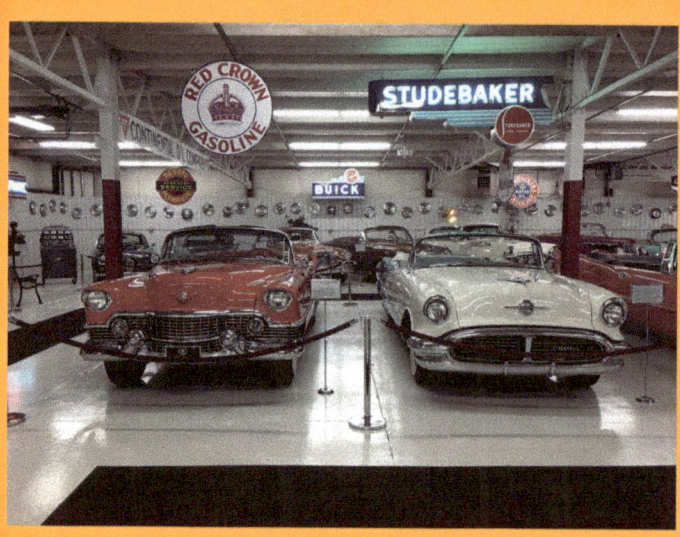

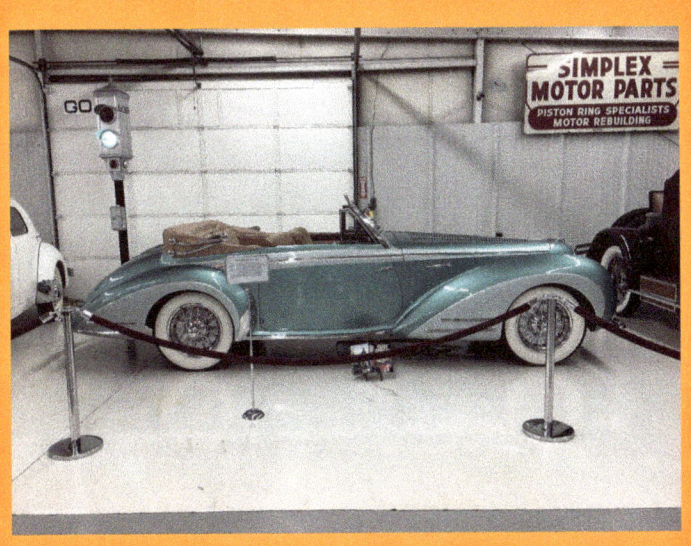

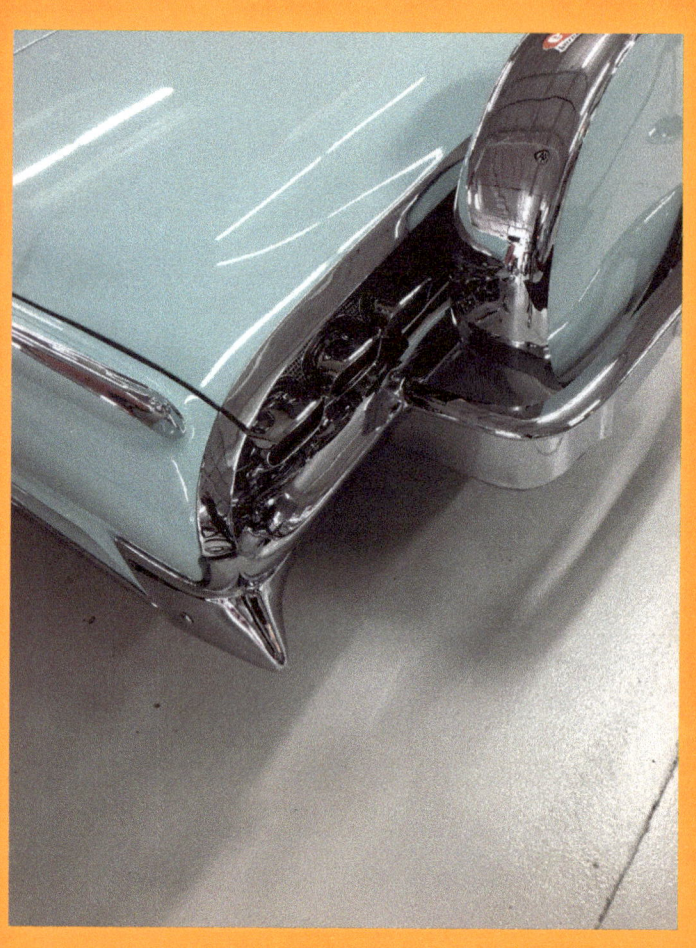

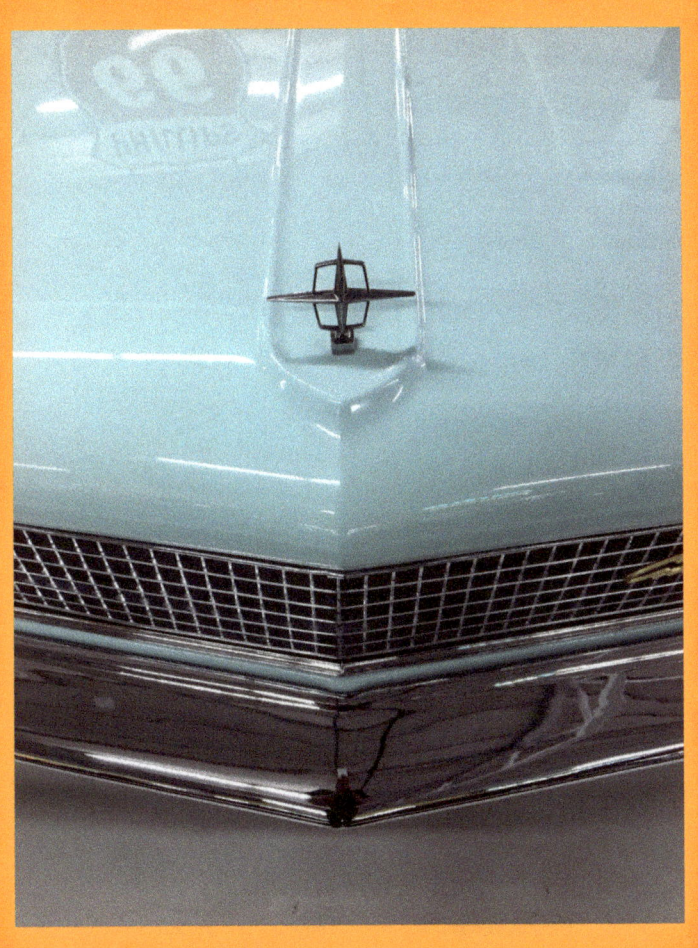

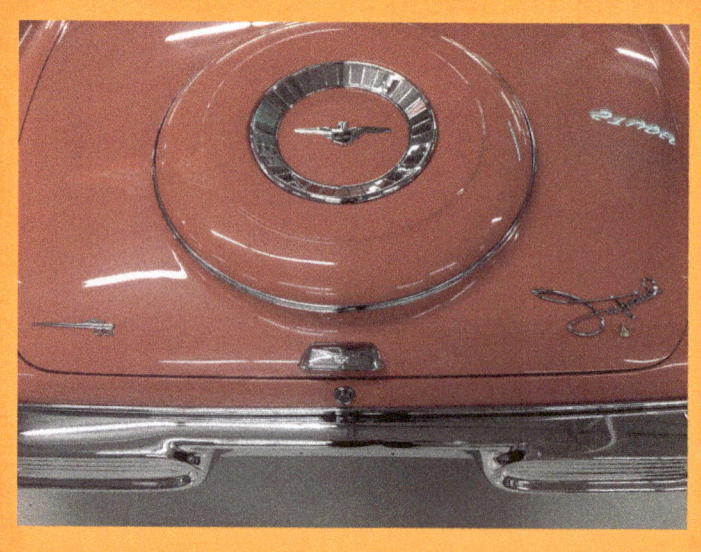

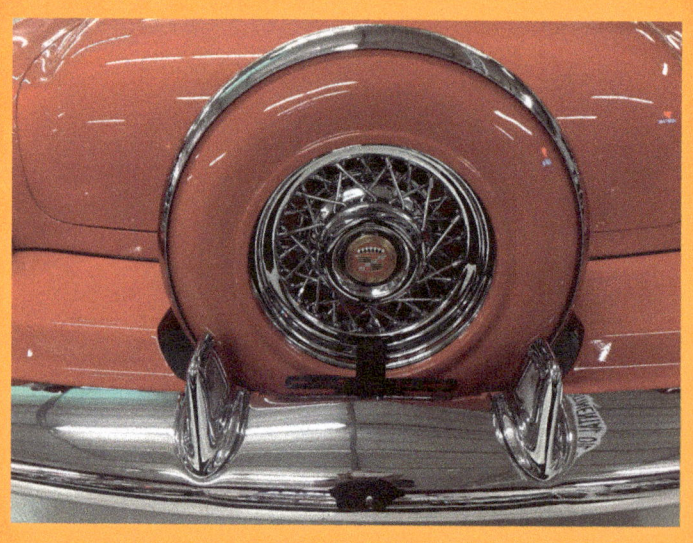

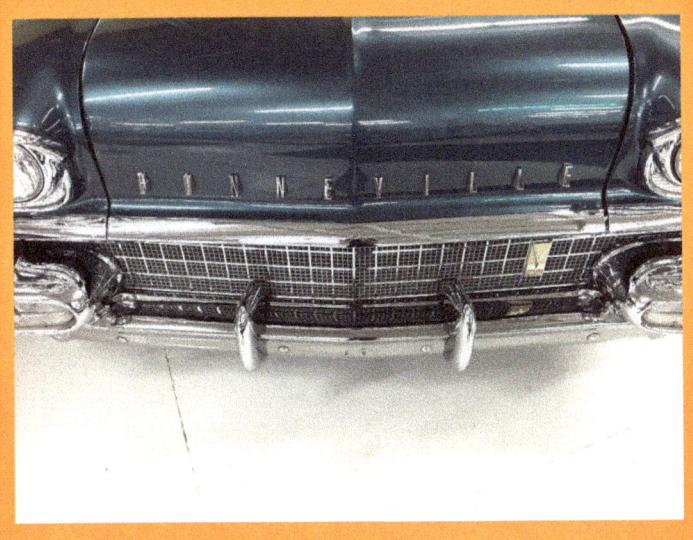

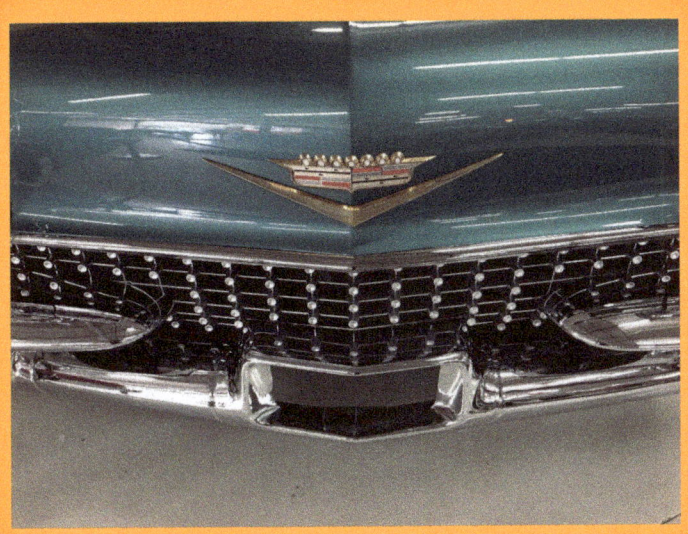

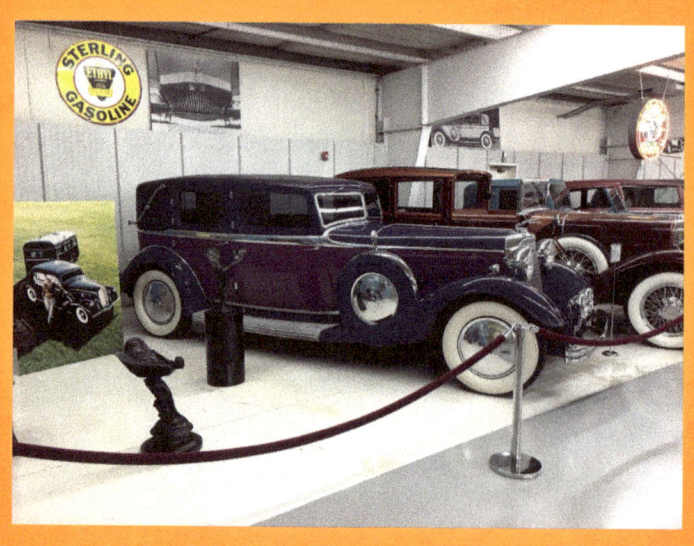

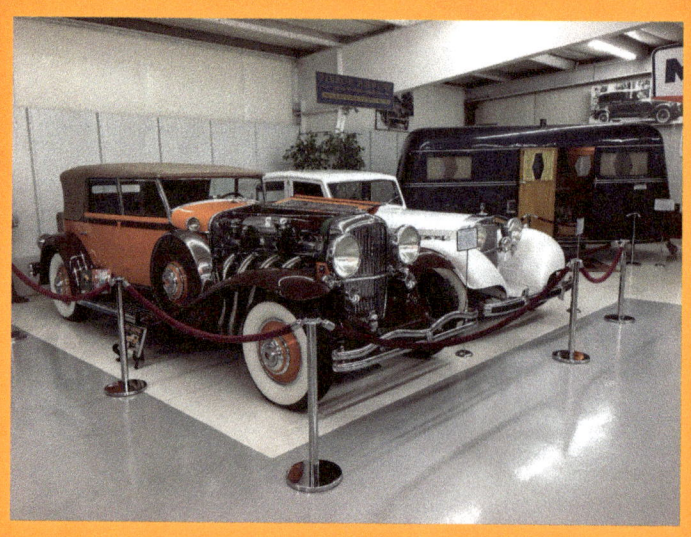

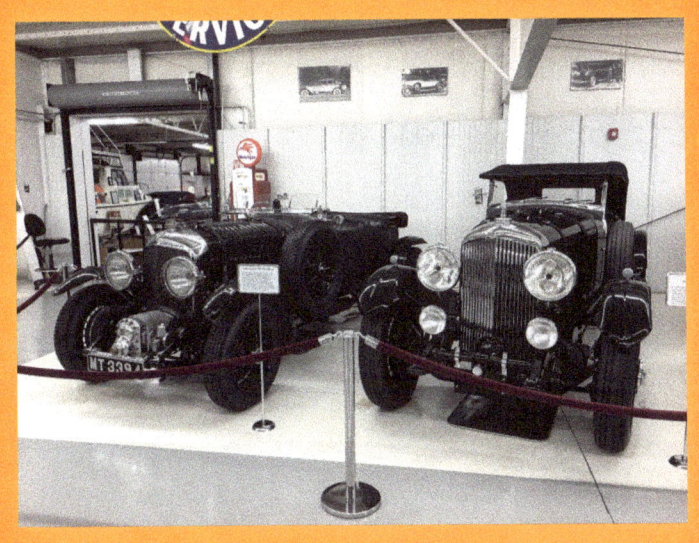

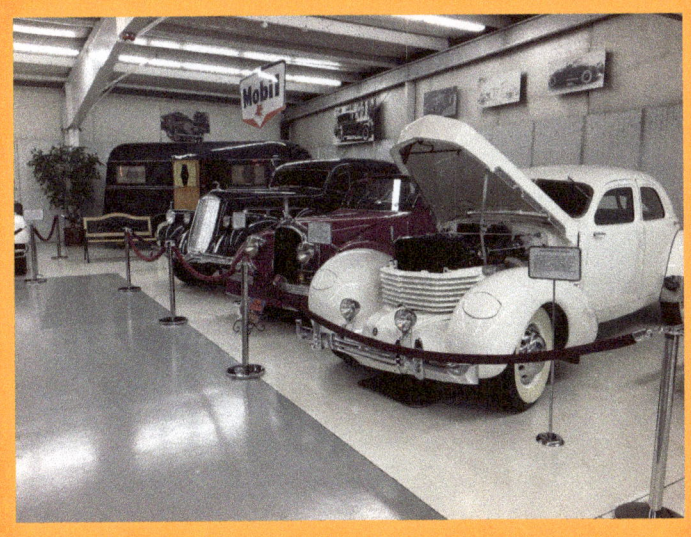

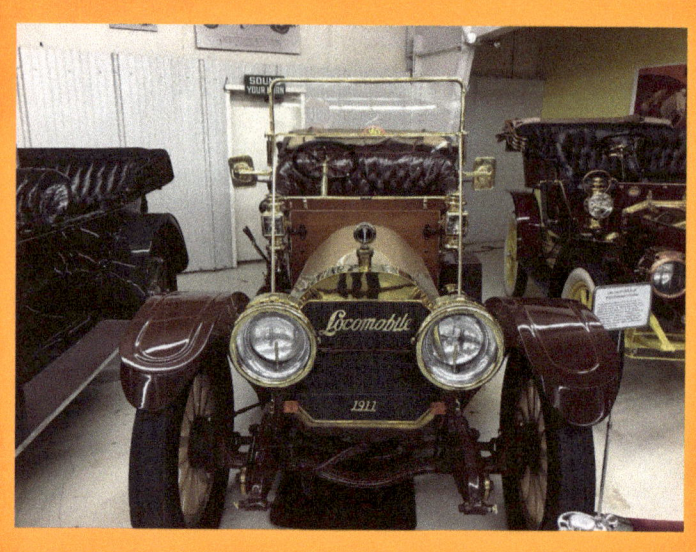

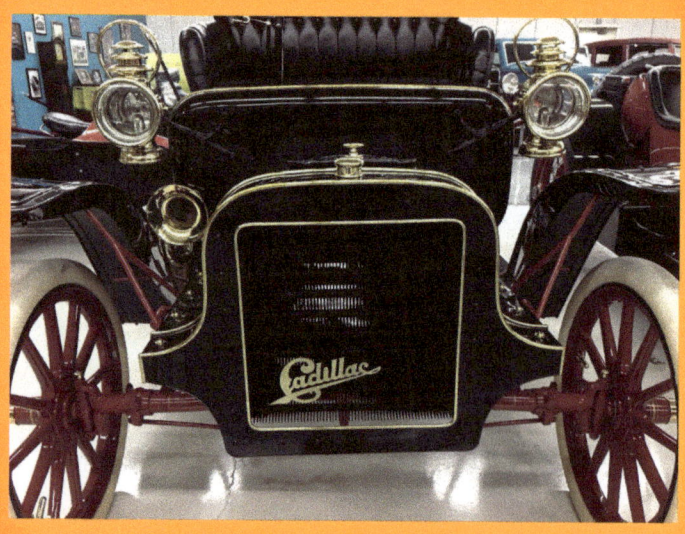

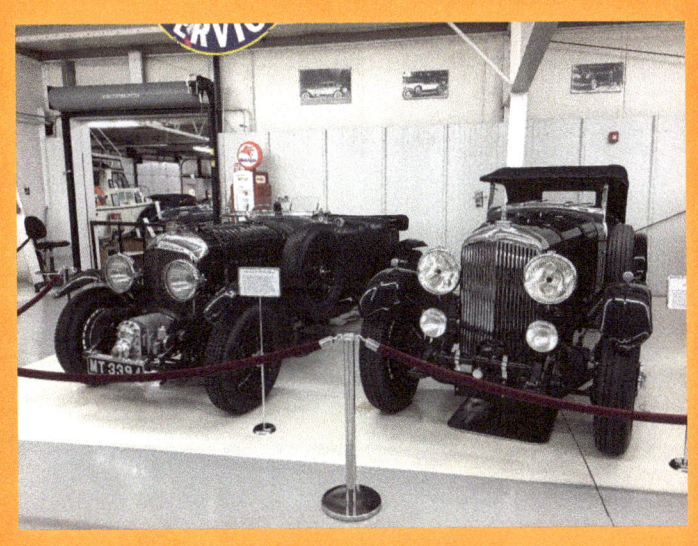

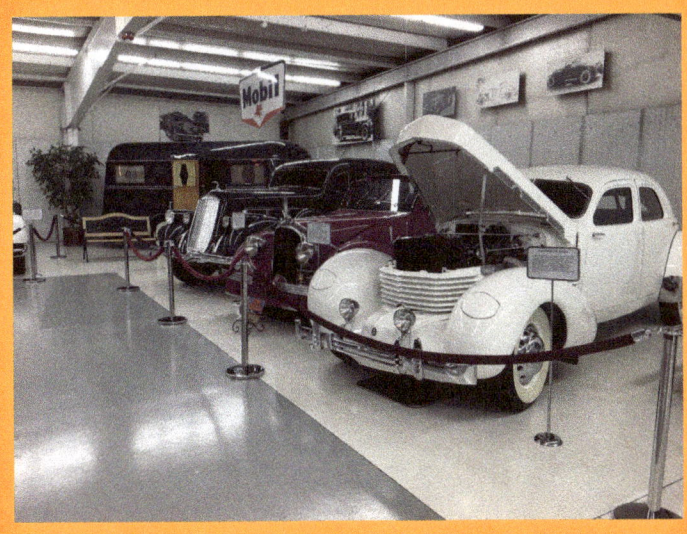

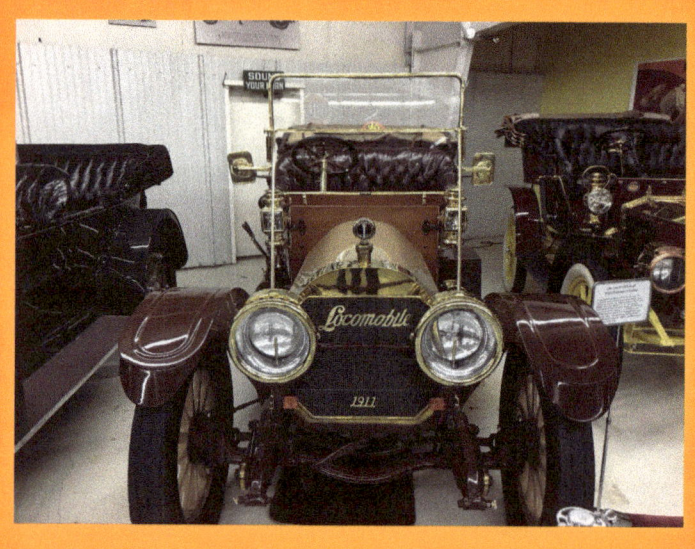

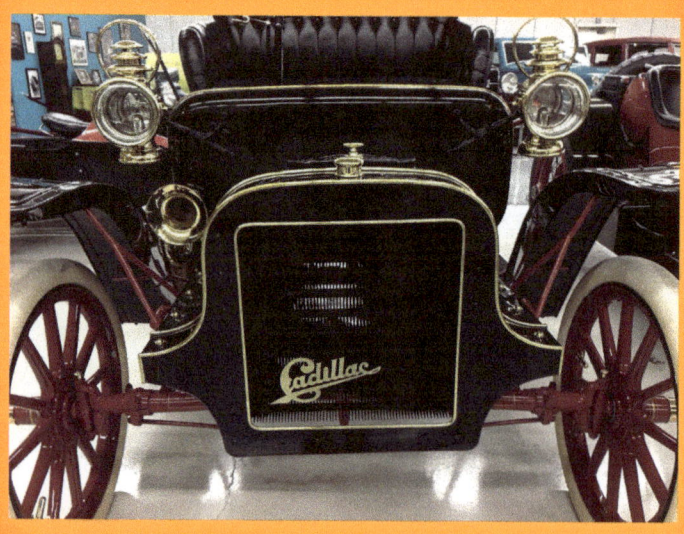

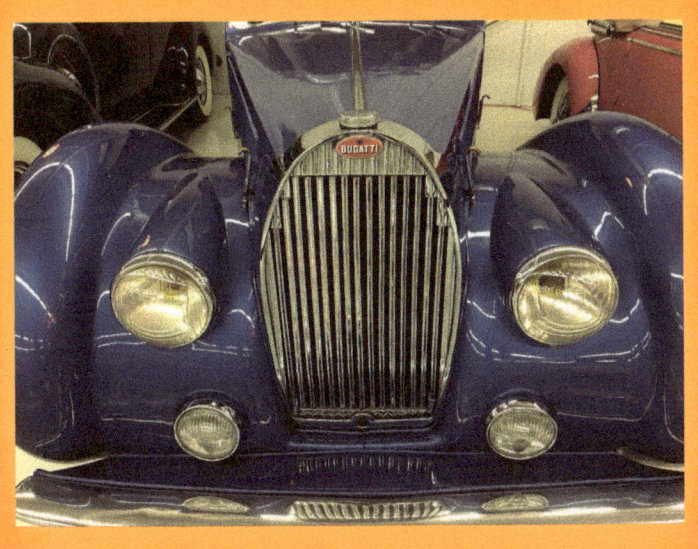

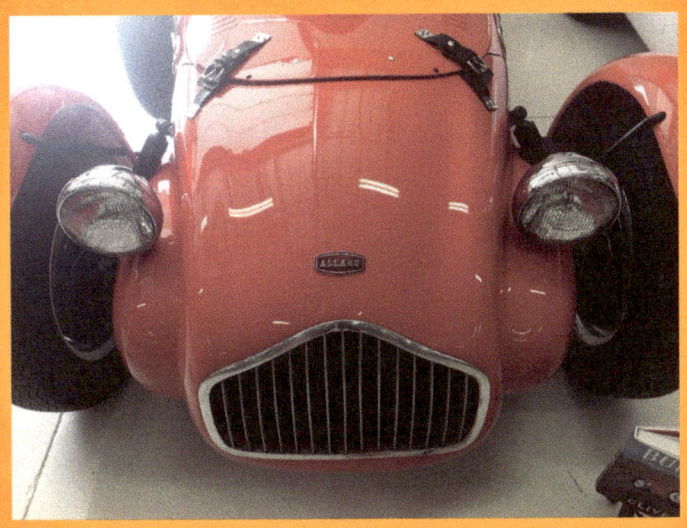

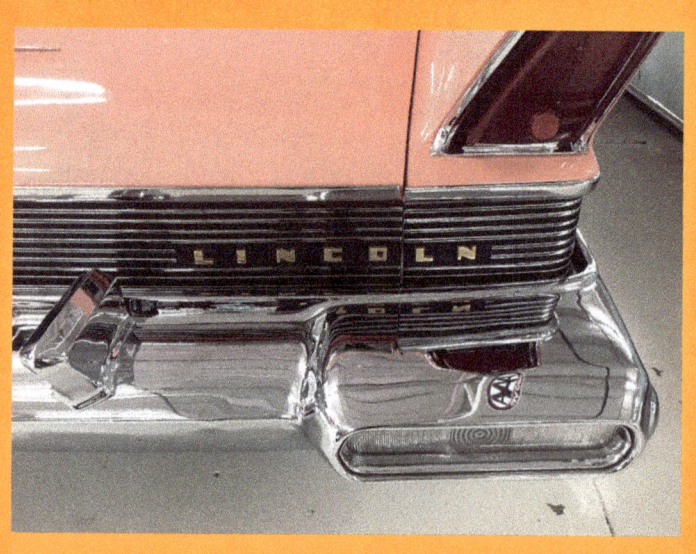

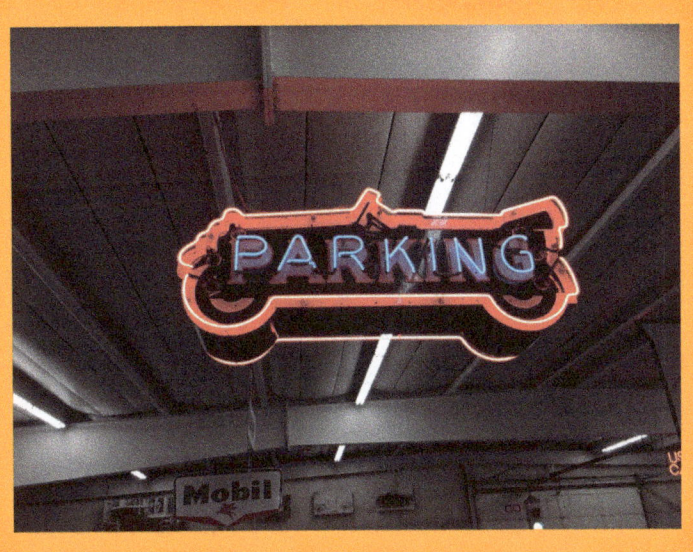

END

END

END

END

END

END

END

666

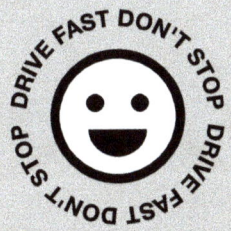

DRIVE FAST DON'T STOP

WWW.DRIVEFASTDONTSTOP.COM

AUTOMOTIVE PHOTO ARCHIVE
BY
MATTHEW JOCELYN

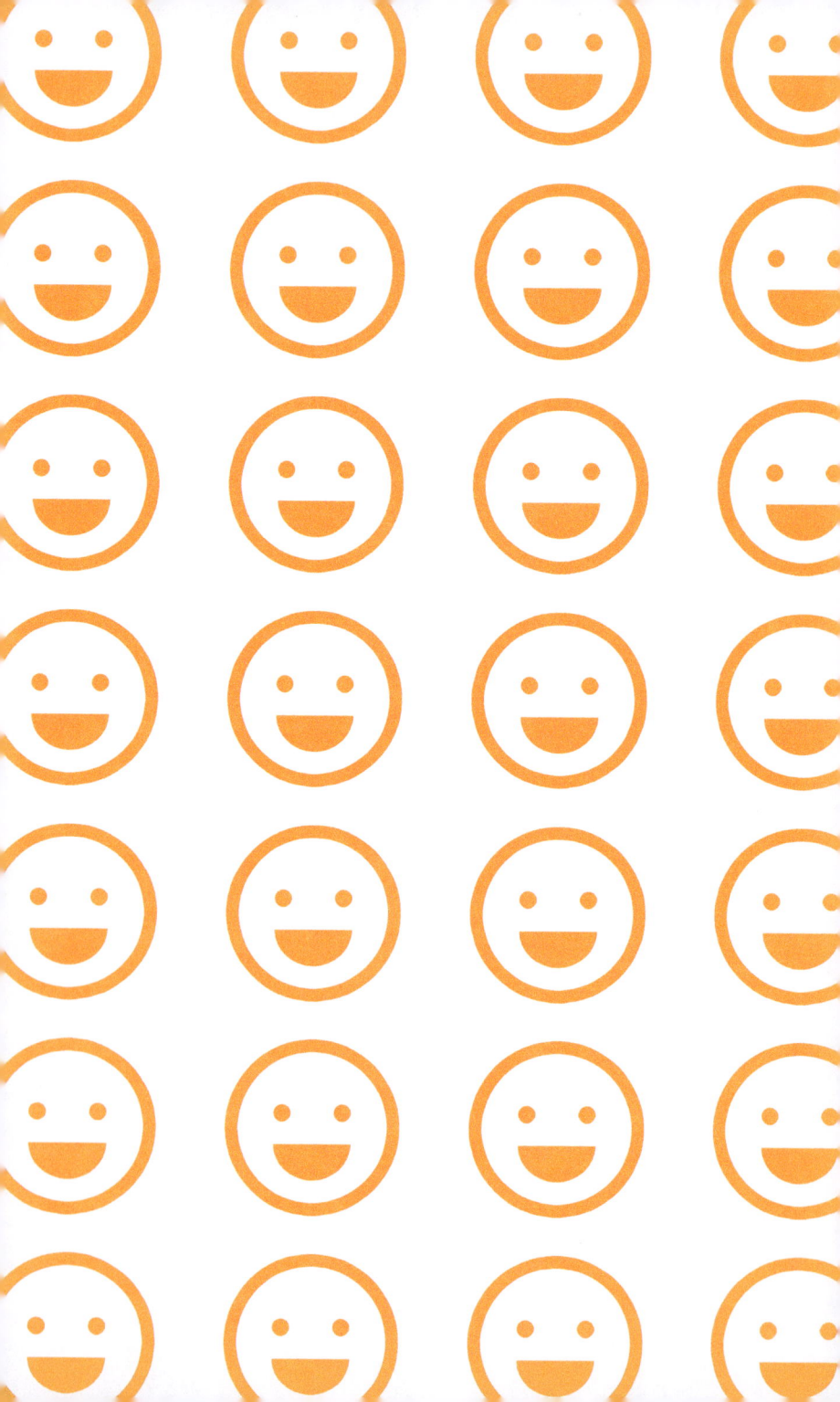

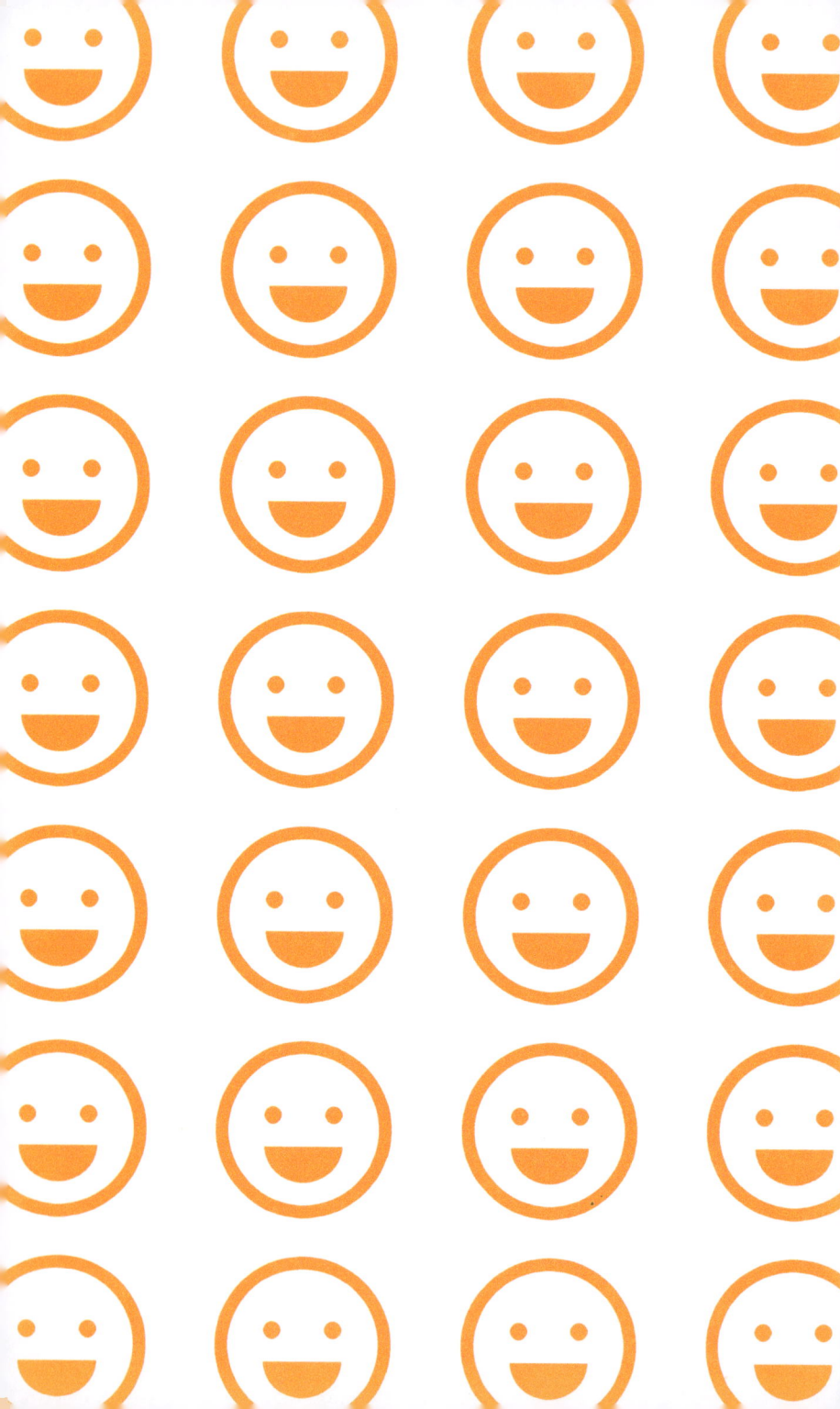